MW00559384

"The continent's greatest clinical psychologist, Diane Ehrensaft, PhD, working in pediatric gender issues in an academic research setting, has added to her two previous groundbreaking books, now with colleague Michelle Jurkiewicz, PsyD. *Gender Explained* reveals how our thinking about gender has changed through the lens and voices of patients, parents, and those who care for gender creative children. In addition to their clinical expertise, Dr. Ehrensaft also draws on her participation in two NIH-funded longitudinal studies of transgender children and adolescents, in collaboration with three other major pediatric academic hospitals."

**—NORMAN SPACK, MD, endocrinologist
at Boston Children's Hospital**

"With courage and wisdom, this book does an amazing job at explaining gender diversity. It brings together empirical research, clinical experience as well as testimonies of children and their parents to answer complicated questions about child and identity development, best parenting approaches and how to understand today's shifting cultural landscape on gender and young people. A highly recommended read for families, clinicians, and anyone eager to better understand our complex world."

**—JEAN MALPAS, psychotherapist and founder of the
Gender & Family Project at the Ackerman Institute for the Family**

"Empathetic and accessible, *Gender Explained* helped me see 'the other side' of the gender debate. It acknowledges the fear and concern that many people face and helps us expand our view of gender. I loved reading it."

—XIMENA LOPEZ, MD, pediatric endocrinologist

"At a time when there is a lot of divisive information and messages on this topic, *Gender Explained* unites us in supporting the health and well-being of all children. Dr. Ehrensaft and Dr. Jurkiewicz provide clear and compassionate information from decades of firsthand experience. This is the perfect book for parents, caregivers, and professionals who are supporting gender expansive children and youth."

—LINDA A. HAWKINS, PhD, director of the Gender & Sexuality Development Program at Children's Hospital of Philadelphia

"A compelling new book rooted in the gender affirmative model, *Gender Explained* provides a nuanced perspective and effectively clarifies some deep misrepresentations of this model. It provides a wealth of information on the care of gender diverse young people."

—AMY TISHELMAN, PhD, Boston College, Department of Psychology and Neuroscience

GENDER EXPLAINED

ALSO BY DIANE EHRENSAFT, PhD

The Gender Creative Child: Pathways for
Nurturing and Supporting Children
Who Live Outside Gender Boxes

Gender Born, Gender Made: Raising Healthy
Gender-Nonconforming Children

Mommies, Daddies, Donors, Surrogates: Answering
Tough Questions and Building Strong Families

Spoiling Childhood: How Well-Meaning
Parents are Giving Children Too Much—
But Not What They Need

Parenting Together: Men and Women Sharing
the Care of their Children

GEN DER

A New Understanding of Identity in a Gender Creative World

EXP LAI NED

DIANE EHRENSAFT, PhD
MICHELLE JURKIEWICZ, PsyD

Foreword by Stephen M. Rosenthal, MD

THE EXPERIMENT

NEW YORK

GENDER EXPLAINED: *A New Understanding of Identity in a Gender Creative World*
Copyright © 2024 by Diane Ehrensaft, PhD, and Michelle Jurkiewicz, PsyD
Foreword copyright © 2024 by Stephen M. Rosenthal, MD

The Experiment, LLC
220 East 23rd Street, Suite 600
New York, NY 10010-4658
theexperimentpublishing.com

The Experiment's books are available at special discounts when purchased in bulk for premiums and sales promotions as well as for fund-raising or educational use. For details, contact us at info@theexperimentpublishing.com.

Library of Congress Cataloging-in-Publication Data

Names: Ehrensaft, Diane, author. | Jurkiewicz, Michelle, author.
Title: Gender explained : a new understanding of identity in a gender
  creative world / Diane Ehrensaft, PhD, Michelle Jurkiewicz, PsyD.
Description: New York : The Experiment, [2024] | Includes bibliographical
  references and index.
Identifiers: LCCN 2024013583 (print) | LCCN 2024013584 (ebook) | ISBN
  9781891011559 (hardcover) | ISBN 9781891011566 (ebook)
Subjects: LCSH: Gender identity. | Gender dysphoria.
Classification: LCC HQ18.55 .E35 2024 (print) | LCC HQ18.55 (ebook) | DDC
  305.3--dc23/eng/20240422
LC record available at https://lccn.loc.gov/2024013583
LC ebook record available at https://lccn.loc.gov/2024013584

ISBN 978-1-891011-55-9
Ebook ISBN 978-1-891011-56-6

Jacket and text design by Jack Dunnington
Author photographs courtesy of the author (Diane Ehrensaft)
and by Ben Krantz Studio (Michelle Jurkiewicz)

Manufactured in the United States of America

First printing August 2024
10 9 8 7 6 5 4 3 2 1

To all the gender creative children and
parents who have taught us so well

Contents

Foreword

by Stephen M. Rosenthal, MD

While gender was once primarily in the domain of psychologists and social scientists, it has found its way into mainstream consciousness. But what is gender, and why, in recent years has it become associated with emotionally charged and heated debate, often landing in the crosshairs of a culture war? This book by Diane Ehrensaft, PhD, and Michelle Jurkiewicz, PsyD, truly lives up to its title, *Gender Explained: A New Understanding of Identity in a Gender Creative World.*

Gender identity, a person's inner sense of self as male, female, or somewhere on the gender spectrum, is typically aligned with a person's sex—the physical or genetic attributes that characterize biological maleness or femaleness; for example, external and internal genital structures, gonads, and sex chromosomes. However, gender and sex are not always aligned, and individuals have demonstrated gender diversity throughout history. The reality that a person's sex and gender can be different has spawned the concept of gender-affirming care, based on the belief that every person is entitled to live in the gender that is most authentic to them, and in a manner that honors a person's individuality and promotes their well-being. What is this care, and why is it so controversial?

While not every gender-diverse person seeks medical and/or surgical treatments to bring their physical sex characteristics into alignment with their gender identity, recent years have borne witness to an increasing number of transgender and gender-diverse youth seeking gender-affirming care—an approach that was pioneered in the Neth-erlands and that only emerged in the late twentieth century.

Through the lens of developmental psychology, Dr. Ehrensaft, an internationally recognized expert in child and adolescent gender care, and her colleague, Dr. Jurkiewicz, carefully guide us on a journey to fully understand gender itself and gender-affirming care. This guidance is re-markably accessible and engaging, as if the authors are speaking directly to you—whether you are a parent/caregiver, client, or provider, or sim-ply a person who wants to learn. The authors address core issues about medical interventions, including puberty blockers, gender-affirming sex hormones, and gender-affirming surgeries—explaining when such treatment is indicated and when it is not—and they thoughtfully tackle every major gender-related controversy of our time: Why the exponen-tial increase in youth referrals to gender clinics, globally, in recent years? Why the increase in gender-diverse adolescents designated female at birth? When do youth know their gender? What is the state of re-search for gender-affirming care for adolescents; what are the risks and benefits of such care; what are the gaps in our knowledge; and what are the barriers to such care? Why the controversy surrounding sports—in particular, participation of transgender girls in girls' sports—and how to think about the challenges in prioritizing inclusion as well as fairness? What are the complexities involved in these considerations? And what about retransition, discontinuation of care, and regret?

In a refreshing and inspiring style, this book teaches us about "gen-der literacy," making the compelling case that learning about gender is lifelong, and that gender is not necessarily fixed at any age, but may, in some, evolve over a lifetime. With the aim of promoting gender health for all—not just adolescents—the authors emphasize the im-portance of "listening, not telling," and by their own examples, they provide guidance on strategies to promote your own self-reflection to enhance your gender literacy. Despite the controversies, we live in a time of evolving research and increased understanding that will be key to optimizing gender-affirming care. *Gender Explained* challenges us to imagine a time when "gender in all its splendor is just a fact of life."

STEPHEN M. ROSENTHAL, MD, is cofounder and medical director of the multidisciplinary UCSF Child and Adolescent Gender Center (CAGC), where he cares for young transgender clients. He also cares for pediatric clients with endocrine disorders, such as abnormalities involving thyroid function or growth and puberty. Dr. Rosenthal is one of four principal investigators for the Impact of Early Medical Treatment in Transgender Youth, a multicenter study sponsored by the National Institutes of Health and the Eunice Kennedy Shriver National Institute of Child Health and Human Development. He is currently a member of the board of directors of the World Professional Association for Transgender Health.

Glossary

Cisgender: A person whose sex designated at birth matches their gender identity.

DFAB: An abbreviated term for "designated female at birth," previously known as "assigned female at birth" (AFAB), referring to a person who is perceived as female at birth.

DMAB: An abbreviated term for "designated male at birth," previously known as "assigned male at birth" (AMAB), referring to a person who is perceived as male at birth.

GAHT (gender-affirming hormone treatment): A medical treatment that provides a person with hormones (i.e., estrogen or testosterone) to treat dysphoria and to align their body more closely with their gender identity.

Gender Creativity: The psychological process by which each individual consolidates their unique gender self, based on nature, nurture, and culture.

Gender Diverse: Used to describe any person who identifies as or expresses their gender in ways that are outside of conventional norms. Some examples include a cisgender man who wears nail polish and long hair or a nonbinary person who presents as androgynous.

Gender Dysphoria: Distress or discomfort that may occur for some people whose gender identity does not match their sex designated at birth.

Gender Expressions: The ways in which a person expresses their gender, such as through clothing, hairstyles, and mannerisms.

Gender Identity: Refers to the gender that a person identifies with. This identity may match their sex designated at birth (i.e., cisgender) or may not match their sex designated at birth (i.e., transgender).

Gender Minority Stress: High levels of stress faced by transgender and gender-diverse people as the result of various social and structural factors, such as poor social support and discrimination.

Gender Noise: Constant thoughts, feelings, or worries about one's gender and how other people are experiencing it, sometimes preoccupying a person or distracting them from other activities.

Genderqueer: A gender identity that cannot be categorized into girl/woman or boy/man.

Gonadotropin-Releasing Hormone (GnRH) Agonists: The medical term for puberty blockers, which are medications that stop the body from producing the hormones (i.e., estrogen or testosterone) that cause the physical changes of puberty.

Nonbinary: A variety of gender identities that do not exclusively fit into girl/woman or boy/man. For example, a person might identify as both a girl and a boy or as neither a girl nor a boy.

Puberty Blockers: Common term for GnRH agonists. See above.

Sex Designated at Birth: The sex (male or female) that a person is designated to be based on their genitals at birth.

Sexual Identity: An identity based on who someone is sexually attracted to, often based on the other's gender identity. Some common sexual identities include heterosexual, gay, lesbian, or bisexual, among others.

Transgender: A person whose gender identity does not match their sex designated at birth.

Transfeminine/Transfemme: Usually a person designated male at birth who identifies as any number of gender identities outside of boy/man, for whom femininity is an important part of their gender identity. For example, someone may identify as nonbinary and transfemme.

Transmasculine/Transmasc: Usually a person designated female at birth who identifies as any number of gender identities outside of girl/woman, for whom masculinity is an important part of their gender identity. For example, someone may identify as nonbinary and transmasc.

Trans Boy/Trans Man: A person who was designated female at birth and identifies as a boy or man.

Trans Girl/Trans Woman: A person who was designated male at birth and identifies as a girl or woman.

CHAPTER 1

Much Ado About Gender

Jenna Karvunidis came up with an idea to celebrate the upcoming birth of her first child, Bianca, born in 2008. She and her husband decided to host an event revealing their baby's gender to family and friends with a special cake that contained colored icing inside—blue for a boy or pink for a girl. Jenna neither intended nor expected that her gender reveal party idea would take off as it did with party packs sold on Amazon, websites devoted to gender reveal party planning, and gender reveal parties featured on popular TV series. Most of these parties have included simple ways of announcing a baby's gender, such as the cake filling that Jenna used, or with the release of balloons: pink for "It's a girl" or blue for "It's a boy."

Unfortunately, some of these parties became so extravagant that gender reveal parties gone horribly wrong made many headlines over the years. For example, in 2017, more than forty-five thousand acres in and around Coronado National Forest burned after an expectant father shot a rifle at a target that contained pink or blue explosive powder, which resulted in damages greater than eight million dollars. Another wildfire started by a gender reveal party in 2020 resulted in the death of a firefighter and criminal charges for the expectant parents. Other gender reveal parties made headlines after serious injuries to partygoers, and in fact, there were at least seven deaths in five separate incidences, including a pilot's death during a gender reveal party stunt in 2023, all in an attempt to celebrate the gender of a child not even born yet.

Over the subsequent years, Jenna had two more children and watched as all of their genders developed. One Christmas morning, her three-year-old middle daughter burst into tears because she thought her Lego set in primary colors was a "boy's toy" and didn't have girly-enough colors. Bianca, for whom Jenna had held the one and only gender reveal party, rejected dresses and preferred to wear a suit for their family photo instead.[1] These two children had very different gender experiences and expressions even though both identified as girls and were raised in the same family. By 2019, Jenna expressed regret for ever starting the gender reveal party trend. In her own words, she stated, "Who cares what gender the baby is? I did at the time because we didn't live in 2019 and didn't know what we know now—that assigning focus on gender at birth leaves out so much of their potential and talents that have nothing to do with what's between their legs."[2]

State of Affairs

As Jenna pointed out, a lot has changed about gender in a relatively short time. Hardly a day goes by across media outlets without reference to a gender-related issue, usually about children and adolescents. Should bathrooms be divided by gender, and if so, which bathroom does a transgender person use? What about a nonbinary person? Which sports team does a transgender or gender-diverse child play on? Should educators have to notify parents if a child starts using different pronouns or is going by a new name at school? Is gender diversity allowed to be discussed in schools, or is it too dangerous? And, perhaps most contentious, what is gender-affirming care and should children have access to it? How old should someone be before starting a medical gender transition, such as hormones or gender-affirming surgery? And who should be in charge of answering these questions? Regardless of how you think and feel about gender, whether you celebrate gender variations or fear these changes are leading to the downfall of civilized society, you are thinking about gender.

Research indicates that the number of transgender youth, aged thirteen to seventeen, in the United States doubled between 2017 and 2020 to three hundred thousand, about 1.4 percent of the youth population.[3] By 2022, the Pew Research Center reported that 5 percent of young adults in the United States identified as a gender other than the sex on their birth certificate. Approximately 2 percent identified as either a trans man (designated female at birth and identifies as a man) or trans woman (designated male at birth and identifies as a woman). The remaining 3 percent reported a nonbinary identity.[4] "Nonbinary" is an umbrella term that can refer to many different experiences of gender identity. Some nonbinary children and youth may identify as feeling like both a boy and a girl, feeling like neither, feeling like sometimes a boy and sometimes a girl, or as something altogether different than boy or girl.

The numbers of transgender and gender-diverse children and teens are reportedly rising, not just in the United States, but around the globe. For example, Latin America as a whole saw the number of transgender people increase by nearly 50 percent between 2008 and 2016.[5] The Tavistock Clinic, the only pediatric gender center in England from 2010 to 2015, saw a yearly 50 percent increase of child and adolescent referrals during that time, and then from 2015 to 2016, the referrals doubled.[6] Similar numbers were reported in Denmark,[7] and during roughly the same time period, Canada reported an increase of ten times the referrals at their gender clinics for children and adolescents.[8]

In response to the increased numbers of transgender and gender-diverse young people and families seeking support for their children, pediatric interdisciplinary gender programs were established. Most of these gender centers are located in major research hospitals and include an interdisciplinary team made up of pediatricians, endocrinologists, social workers, psychiatrists, and psychologists. Children and their families are helped by an entire team and are provided with comprehensive gender care, including information, medical care, mental health care, and aid in accessing additional services such as educational and legal supports. The number of these clinics continues to grow in an attempt to meet the demand. In the United States, for example, the number of gender clinics increased from an initial four to at least sixty within a decade. Yet, despite the rapid growth in gender services, the existing pediatric clinics throughout the world are often overwhelmed with referrals exceeding their capacity. This results in long waitlists, but only for those privileged enough to access care, proving to be another significant barrier for families without the health insurance coverage, money, or location to access gender care for their children.

A Gender Debate

Gender is increasingly politicized as governments on every continent (except Antarctica) attempt to govern and legislate gender, with a particular focus on children, youth activities, and access to gender-affirming care. Not only governments, but local school boards have moved to regulate gender in schools from kindergarten through twelfth grade in the United States—who should get to use which bathrooms, what books should be in the library or on the reading lists, who gets to participate in girls' and boys' sport teams and extracurricular events, and in some cases, even what can be discussed between a teacher and a student. This legislation negatively impacts students. Spencer, a sixteen-year-old in Tennessee, described fear of using the boys' bathroom at his high school because of who he might encounter and how they might treat him. Spencer was designated male at birth, uses he/him pronouns, but often wears dresses and makeup. At the time, Tennessee state law included strict gender mandates: That a student was permitted to play sports only on the team that matched their sex designated at birth regardless of their gender identity, therefore transgender and gender-diverse students were prohibited from teams that aligned with their gender identity. There were also increased demands to ban books that discuss sexual orientation or gender identity, and in Spencer's school district, even to ban books that simply include LGBTQ+ characters. In the midst of this turmoil, Spencer started a pride club at school with the hope of providing a safe space for

LGBTQ+ students. Yet, despite their best efforts, Spencer and the student pride club were booed at the homecoming parade *by adults*. In reference to the proposed bans and to the manner in which LGBTQ+ students are treated, Spencer stated, "People should know that no matter what bill they try to pass or book they try to ban or thing they try to ban teachers or students from talking about in schools, it doesn't change who people are, and it doesn't change who we're going to continue to be."[9] Tennessee's complete ban on gender-affirming medical care went into effect July 1, 2023, a little over a year later. This did not bode well for reducing Spencer's anxieties.

Furthermore, attempts have even been made to regulate what constitutes gender-inclusive language and how and where it is used, such as recognizing the pronouns that a person uses rather than the ones that were designated at birth (if different). For example, controversy abounds among English-speaking people in regard to the use of "they" to refer to a single person whose gender is not male or female, or whose gender is not known, or for a person who doesn't believe gender should pertain at all to anyone's pronouns. In light of the fact that "they" as a singular pronoun has been endorsed among many academic circles, publishers, and even the Merriam-Webster dictionary,[10] resistance to the use of "they" as a gender pronoun is alive and well. Even in everyday English, people often use "they" as a singular pronoun, such as in "Someone left *their* keys here. I am sure *they* will be back as soon as *they* realize." Yet, when used in reference to a transgender or gender-diverse person, there are objections that the singular use of "they" is grammatically incorrect English. In fact, some people and institutions refuse to even recognize or use someone's pronouns if the individual uses anything outside of he/him and she/her.

Even more controversial are debates concerning languages that divide words into masculine or feminine categories, such as romance languages. For example, there is an attempt to make Spanish more gender-neutral by replacing designated feminine words (ending in "a") or masculine (ending in "o") with the ending "e," albeit that this shift significantly changes the language spoken by over half a billion people.

Some governments in Latin America, such as Argentina, have pushed to outlaw the use of gender-neutral language changes, particularly within the school systems, and these attempts to block the change were promptly met with fierce protests among youth.

Furthermore, some countries or states are imposing definitions as to what defines "legitimate" gender identities, often dictating that a child can be only a boy or a girl determined by their genitals at birth, such as in the UK, where the government recognizes only male and female genders. Several other countries offer recognition of a third gender, such as the United States, which recognizes the gender "X" on US passports for those who identify outside of the male or female designated to them at birth. Similar policies are found in countries ranging from Canada to Australia to India, where a third gender option was implemented after their supreme court stated that, "It is the right of every human being to choose their gender."[11]

Even in countries where protection and care increased for gender-diverse people over the last decade, the debate has become so contentious that legislators passed (or attempted to pass) laws banning or severely limiting access to gender-affirming care in the name of "protecting children." For perhaps the first time ever in the United States, measures promoted by some politicians to deny evidence-based gender-affirming health care to children and youth are in direct contradiction to the recommendations of the American Medical Association (AMA), the American Psychological Association (APA), the American Academy of Pediatrics (AAP), and many more professional organizations made up of experts in the field of pediatric gender care. In other words, certain legislators want the power to make health care decisions for children and their families while disregarding the expertise of trained health care providers and the science on which those experts base their practices. In fact, the debate about gender-affirming care has become so controversial and sensationalized in the media that there is now widespread confusion about what "gender-affirming care" even means, which we hope to clarify in the upcoming pages of this book.

Child and Adolescent Mental Health

As the controversy around gender and pediatric gender care swirls around us, the rates of child and adolescent anxiety, depression, Attention Deficit Hyperactivity Disorder (ADHD), Post-Traumatic Stress Disorder (PTSD), sleep disorders, suicidal behaviors, addiction disorders, and other psychosocial problems are at unprecedented heights around the world, particularly after the COVID-19 pandemic.[12] Suicide is the fourth leading cause of death among young people ages fifteen to nineteen worldwide. In the United States specifically, suicide is the *third* leading cause of death ages fifteen to nineteen, and the *second* leading cause of death among those ages ten to fourteen.[13] In fact, the Centers for Disease Control and Prevention (CDC) in the United States reported that the suicide rate among fourteen- to eighteen-year-olds rose by an astounding 61.7 percent from 2009 to 2018.[14] In England, the suicide rates among youth ages fifteen to nineteen rose by 35 percent during 2020 to 2021 to the highest number in the preceding thirty years.[15]

The fact that youth suicide rates are the highest among transgender and gender-diverse youth, specifically among those gender-diverse children and teenagers who experience rejection or a lack of support from their families and immediate communities, is well-documented. In some of the most concerning cases, family rejection leaves youth unhoused and contributes to the fact that transgender youth are at a much higher risk of housing instability than their cisgender peers, often because they are no longer welcome in their family homes. Unhoused transgender youth are also at higher risk of victimization, substance use disorders, and other psychosocial problems than cisgender homeless youth.[16] While these facts are deeply concerning, research demonstrates potential protective factors for transgender and gender-diverse children, with one of the strongest mitigating factors being family acceptance.[17] We will delve into what family acceptance is in chapter 7 because, contrary to some beliefs, it does not mean just doing whatever a child wants. Given these serious risks, it is crucial to identify what these children and youth need to thrive and to take steps to support them and their families.

Gender as a Bedrock

For so many of us, gender has been experienced as an immutable bedrock, remaining steady throughout a lifetime. It has been an organizing principle in cultures around the world for millennia. The sex designated at birth dictated much about a child's future, including the opportunities available to them, the roles they would play at home and in society, and the expectations and standards their community would hold them to. A baby's gender would influence and shape their temperament, personality features, and inclinations. Everyone knew what to expect from this baby and from each other in the most general and fundamental sense. Perhaps this is why gender reveal parties caught on so quickly— because gender seemed the perfect way to introduce a new member of the family or community. For millennia, gender represented an essential feature explaining who a baby was before they were even born, and therefore, the community could welcome in a known being with a foreseeable future rather than facing a stranger. Now, gender as we have known it is suddenly upended—there is no more gender in just two boxes, no more accuracy in gender reveal parties, no more blue for boys and pink for girls. What's more, the critical movers and shakers in these "no mores" are the youngest generations, some as young as two years old, some just old enough to vote or be considered legal adults.

In the midst of this gender shake-up, many people desperately looking for a stabilizing toehold grab at ready answers to the looming questions: What is going on here—whatever happened to boys will be boys and girls will be girls? Why are so many youth saying, "I'm not the gender you thought I was"? Is it social media or social isolation? Social contagion or peer pressure? Is it rooted in parenting or liberal politics? And whatever is to be done about it? As we look around the globe, we find ourselves in a polarized situation—people have been caught up in two increasingly opposing sides of this gender controversy and are becoming more entrenched in their differing narratives, closing down any opportunities to listen to each other. Each side points blame at the other for the verifiable plight of transgender and gender-diverse youth. On one end of the spectrum are those who, in defense of traditional notions of gender, accuse the other side of child abuse when boys are allowed to be girls and girls to be boys. They insist that if access to gender-affirmative care is permitted, it will likely cause irreversible damage. On the other end are those who insist on following the lead of the younger generation. They point back and argue that to refuse youth access to gender-affirming care or to prohibit them from living in their authentic gender is the actual child abuse, putting children at risk for compromised mental health or even worse.

To add fuel to the fire, unfounded theories and misinformation fill in the gaps of our knowledge and muddy the waters as we grapple with these questions. We witness politicians or journalists who cite "experts" who often do not even work in the field of pediatric gender care to make their case against gender-affirming care. What's science, what's myth? What's fact, what's fiction? Navigating this polarized world of gender creates anything but a favorable milieu in which to find not just a foothold, but a path forward as we prepare our children for adulthood. As we watch all this, not just from the sidelines but as two psychologists in the field, we are acutely aware of the confusion so many of you are wrestling with as you seek to understand what's going on around you. The misinformation presented in the media creates an unnecessary and added burden to those already carrying so much. As we listen to how pundits talk about gender-diverse youth and their families, we feel compelled to speak up, not just for them, but because of the significant negative impacts these tropes can have on all children, youth, and their families. And so this book was born, to share what we've learned about gender. We invite you to think about what you know about gender as well. If everyone can do this, no one will be left to grab at a branch to avoid a gender free-fall, but instead, we may discover a solid pathway forward, maybe even a new bedrock of gender to replace the old.

Parenting Gender

Parenting in the midst of increased gender diversity can be particularly challenging. One mother wrote the following to an advice column.

My darling girl, my only child, is now a "they," with a very masculine appearance, and a new life that is unfamiliar to all I know. I felt lost, bewildered, and deeply sad when they came out, and I have not been able to recover. What makes it all so much worse is that I feel extremely guilty about my sadness, and afraid that any acknowledgment of it, even inadvertently, will immediately label me a transphobe, which I am not. . . . I do not want to move through my last years despondent and jealous of all the families not contending with this issue—yes, I will say it— the cisgender families with cisgender children. I do not want to cringe every time I see my child. I want to embrace, to feel bold, fierce, and proud of my child and myself. However, I do not see a way out of this dark place. Can you help?[18]

We are particularly mindful of what all this gender shake-up is like for parents. The example above is only one of a multitude of possible experiences that parents have in relation to their child's gender identity and gender expression. If you are a parent, you may be totally confused as you experience what may feel like being trapped between two out-of-sync stereo speakers—one blasts that gender beyond two boxes is all good, the other declares that such foolery will send us to hell in a handbasket. Numerous parents come to us with predicaments—How do I provide the best support possible to my child while protecting them from harm? I want to support my child to be their unique self, whatever their gender is. I want my child to be happy, but what if this is just a phase? Isn't that what childhood or adolescence is all about—discovering one's identity? What if I support their new gender identity, but it turns out to not be who they really are? What if my teen finds themselves having to live as someone they are not? What if they get hurt in a world out there that is not ready to embrace them for who they are? What if my child is exposed to other kids who are experimenting with their gender and my kid gets caught up in the social excitement of it all and wants to try it out for themselves? How do I protect them from the potential negative influence of social media and the social influencers out there? Are my complicated and nuanced feelings OK, and what do I do with them?

All feelings are OK and to be expected. All of your thoughts and questions are valid and important. They require tremendous thoughtfulness. There are no simple answers because every child and family presents with a slightly different situation and context, so what works in one household may not in another. Yet, we do provide a lot of information and research about how to best support both children and parents. Our best hope is that this book will guide you toward answers to all of these questions or help you sort out the answers for yourselves as you reflect on your own experiences.

Quieting the Noise

We (Diane and Michelle) are two clinical psychologists from two different generations, immersed in the field of pediatric gender care for the past thirty-five and fifteen years respectively, and have been watching this explosion go off. We feel an urgency to provide families and the general public with accurate information about this new gender upsurge because there are copious amounts of misinformation without regard to research or practice. We hear it from families who contact us for help, confused because of what they heard and/or read. We hear it from our professional colleagues who are not trained in pediatric gender care but find that many of their young clients are gender diverse, and they want to know how to better understand and best support them. Therefore, the purpose of this book is to share what we've learned. We wish to highlight we are all still in the process of learning about this significant shift from the social bedrock of gender in two boxes (i.e., male and female) to the new ever-expanding permutations and combinations of gender, particularly among the next generations.

We call on our combined years of experiences as clinical psychologists and mental health gender specialists, the voices of the youth themselves, and the constantly evolving research and writing on gender and gender development to write this book with an aim of quieting the cacophony. We will do our best to sort truth from misconceptions, misinformation, and disinformation as we strive to build gender literacy so that more people can be equipped to think and act from a place of comprehension and understanding.

What is gender literacy? The term is taken from University of Minnesota's Gender-Affirmative Life Span Approach.[19] Gender literacy is like learning to read. We first learn the alphabet, then to string letters into words, and words into sentences, and sentences into increasingly complex structures and ideas. We are always expanding our literacy beyond the beginning of A = apple. Applying that concept to gender, gender literacy includes the ever-growing ability to identify social and cultural gender norms, to understand the consequences faced when one steps outside of these norms, and to think critically about gender messaging. It builds the capacity to use this information to develop one's own values and beliefs in regard to gender.[20]

As the book unfolds, we will strive to balance objectivity and subjectivity, cite research, and state the facts as we know them, while also holding a stance that gender diversity is something to be celebrated. We do understand that this is likely new ground for many people, in which case this book may require a big shift in thinking. Therefore, we will clarify our approach along the way and cite some of the research and experiences our stance is based on. Hopefully by the completion of this book, you will feel armed with a greater understanding of gender, the ways it is shifting, and the rubrics of pediatric gender-affirming care in order to make your own informed decisions regarding gender.

We will provide you with gender terms and language, some of which might be new. Significantly, the language of gender is constantly changing and updating. For example, for many years we referred to a transgender boy as a child "assigned female at birth" (AFAB) and a transgender girl as a child "assigned male at birth" (AMAB). While you will still see these terms used in other places, in this book, we have replaced these terms with "designated female at birth" (DFAB) or "designated male at birth" (DMAB). There has been a shift in favor of the word "designated" because, for some, "designation" suggests a more deliberate assignment. People may also use "recorded" at birth, in an attempt to emphasize the reality that this is the gender recorded on legal paperwork. Terms around gender continue to evolve as people increasingly seek accurate language to describe their experiences.

Throughout the book, we have used the voices and stories of children and youth as much as we were able. When these voices and stories were shared with us directly (as opposed to located in published media) we took great care to disguise the identities of these young people. This is not because they are hiding—in fact, many of them are out and proud of their identities—but because we feel protective of them in a time that has become more unsafe for transgender and gender-diverse communities.

As you will see throughout the book, most of our stories and statistics originate in the United States. This is not because these issues are unique to the United States, but because this is where we live and practice. We will do our best to include international information where we can, and in our experience, the issues surrounding gender in children and youth in the United States are consistent with many of the discussions occurring around the world. So, no matter who you are—a parent, teacher, provider, student, or curious onlooker—and no matter where you are, we hope that the following chapters will provide a greater understanding of what *is* happening among young people regarding gender and how deepening our understanding of gender and identity may benefit all of us. In essence, we hope to offer you, our reader, more stable ground to stand on and more security that we are all in this together.

What to Expect in This Book

How and why are gender norms shifting *now*? Chapter 2 will answer this question by examining the change occurring among the youngest generations by placing gender norms in social and historical context. We will demonstrate how these cultural shifts have been building up for decades to allow young people today to reject previous binary gender boxes and create new models of gender that go beyond jumping from a girl box to a boy box or vice versa. These models include expansive identities that cannot be contained in a box at all, such as nonbinary or genderqueer. Even Bianca, mentioned at the beginning of the chapter, is a good example of a gender-diverse youth. While identified with the sex designated to her at birth, she performed her identity in a way that challenges stereotypical ways of presenting as a girl. In fact, in our clinical practices, we have seen a significant rise in those who identify and express their gender in much more fluid and unique ways. This chapter demonstrates how the bedrock of gender norms in our society is shifting from binary gender identities of boy/girl to a much broader spectrum, and how youth are taking the opportunity during this foundational shift to develop their own ideas and norms about gender.

Next, in chapter 3, we take a deeper look into the global anxiety created by the gender explosion. It is understandable that adults, institutions, and governments are feeling anxious, because if gender is no longer a basis of our social order, the very ground that we stand on can feel precarious. We will look at the roots of this global anxiety to understand what feeds it and how it impacts children and youth. Chapter 3 will further look into the distress of transgender and gender-diverse children and youth, who contend with their own anxiety, gender stress, and the impacts of discrimination, in addition to the everyday stresses of growing up in a rapidly changing world. Finally, we will examine how social and cultural anxiety and adults' fears contribute to the distress of children and adolescents and the need to lower everyone's anxiety in order to improve the psychological well-being of all children and youth.

Chapter 4 illustrates what the gender-affirmative model is, what constitutes gender-affirming care, who the providers are, and how the model evolved in response to previous models for providing care for children and youth, such as "watchful waiting" or "learn to live in your own skin." We document the ascent of this model as the prevailing model of care in the United States, Canada, the United Kingdom, and many other countries due to increasing research and positive evidence that gender-affirming care both decreases distress and increases well-being among gender-diverse children and youth. Furthermore, we examine the controversy surrounding this model and directly challenge the myths and misinformation perpetuated in the media in order to equip people with the knowledge to make well-informed decisions for themselves and their families.

Chapter 5 explores the buzz around some statistics that suggest an impressively larger number of youth designated female at birth present as transgender or gender diverse as opposed to those designated male at birth. In fact, the buzz has created such a stir that entire books are dedicated to this phenomenon, perpetuating panic, and are written by people such as journalists with no professional experience in pediatric gender care. There are people who suggest that "girls" are suffering from internalized misogyny remedied by this new "craze," and therefore transform themselves into the more "powerful" gender (i.e., male). Other pundits and politicians opine with the implicit bias that "girls" cannot possibly know their own mind at such a young age, since they are and always have been highly suggestible. Still others insist it is social media and social contagion to blame. In this chapter, we look at the actual numbers and where they come from, explore the accuracy of the reports and public accounts, and offer additional information and perspectives to answer the important question, "Where have all the young girls gone?"

Chapter 6 takes up the question "Do we listen to what children are telling us?" Jenna, mentioned at the beginning of this chapter, acknowledged that her daughter Bianca helped educate her on gender when she stated, "She's [Bianca] more of the gender expert than me. I'm just taking her lead."[21] To mirror Jenna's experience, this chapter highlights the main source of our gender education: listening to the children. Therefore, we turn to accounts of children and youth's experiences in the gender-shifting world. We share stories about a child who has been gender creative from their earliest years, and a child who may not be exploring their own gender but is tuned into the culture's new ideas about the variations of gender identity (who do I feel myself to be?) and gender expressions (how I "do" my gender through observable aspects such as clothing and hairstyles), among others. The second part of the chapter looks at child development and what children need from adults in order to be secure in who they are.

Parents and caregivers often wonder: How do I raise my child to be their best and most authentic self while also keeping them safe and healthy? Chapter 7 reflects on the challenges in raising a child in this new and ever-evolving world in an attempt to answer this question. We highlight how parents work to navigate all the opposing messages and ideological rifts that surround raising a gender-healthy child, just as more and more children challenge them and previous gender norms in new and creative ways. We share what we've learned from the parents we work with: how they respond and relate to their children to ensure they are gender-healthy rather than gender-stressed. We delve into what it means for parents to be the experts of their children while, at the same time, having potential blind spots; how parents affirm their child's gender in ways that feel right to the child; and strategies that parents use to teach gender literacy in order to contribute to building a gender-accepting world.

Chapter 8 investigates some of the largest gender conundrums—gender diversity in sports, education, and medicine. The first half of the chapter examines gender diversity in athletics and classrooms to explore questions such as: Should transgender children and youth be permitted to play sports, and if so, on which teams? What is gender ideology and is it being taught in public schools? What about parental rights? The second half of the chapter goes into gender-affirming social transition and medical care. We address potential risks and benefits as we see them and offer information about how decisions are often made regarding social and medical transitions for our gender creative children and youth. We answer important questions such as: When should a child socially transition? Are puberty blockers safe? Does gender-affirming medical care render youth infertile?

Next, in chapter 9, we turn our focus inward to reflect on the additional work that each of us can do within ourselves. Every person has a gender, and so we begin this chapter with an emphasis on becoming more aware of our own thoughts, feelings, and attitudes about gender, gender diversity, and the changes that reside in each of us, including those of which we have not previously been aware. We explore how gender messages have created expansion in our lives and where they have restricted each one of us. These messages might include "Girls are less apt in science," "It's weird for boys to wear nail polish," or "Transgender boys are not 'real' males; transgender girls are not 'real' females." We also examine how to continue building a gender-inclusive world as a lifelong learner.

Finally, in chapter 10, we step outside of ourselves and our immediate families to the community level so that we can explore what we can do with all that we've learned. It will be a moment to now reflect: Has gender been explained? And we close the pages of this book by peering out onto the horizon to anticipate what may be coming next in these changing times and what else about gender will need explaining. Let the journey begin.

CHAPTER 2

Why Is Gender a Thing for So Many Kids?

I (Michelle) was working in a preschool classroom with a new group of children. One child had short hair and wore a dress with pink, sparkly shoes. When I referred to this child as "she," the other children started laughing hysterically. The children said, "That's not a girl, that's a boy!" as though it were the silliest mistake in the world to think that someone was a girl just because he wore a dress.

GENDER IN OUR SOCIETY LOOKS DIFFERENT TODAY than it did when we began working in pediatric gender care, and it has particularly undergone changes in the last decade. Earlier in our practices, parents brought their young children in to see us because the children were insisting that they were the other gender. These children would assert, "I'm a girl" or "I'm a boy" and most often presented with stereotypical traits and interests of their stated gender. For example, they often primarily had friends of the opposite sex, preferred clothing or toys stereotypically associated with that sex, and wanted to have haircuts that reflected their girlness or boyness in stereotypical ways. Most of these children were designated male at birth, many of whom arrived as boys who wanted to wear dresses and play with dolls, fairy figurines, and plastic mermaids with glimmering tails.

Parents came to us with anxieties about how their girly boys or their transgender daughters might be perceived and treated by others. Should they allow their child to wear a dress? Should they take away all the dolls? While there were also transgender boys, these parents and their children visited us less often, perhaps because these parents understood their child as simply a tomboy. After all, it is more socially acceptable for a little girl to act like a boy than it is for a little boy to act like a girl.

Regardless, gender was understood as binary, meaning that there were only two possibilities. One could fit into either a girl box or a boy box. The girl box was and continues to be larger and more flexible, meaning that it allows for more diverse gender expressions, such as girls doing and wearing what has stereotypically been "boy" activities and clothes. Girls can and do wear pants, grow up to be surgeons or managers, and play sports. In contrast, the boy box was and continues to be more restrictive. Stepping outside it can quickly lead to pejorative names, such as "sissy," or gay slurs.

What If Someone Doesn't Feel Like a Boy or a Girl?

Now the children who arrive in our offices often don't feel like a boy or a girl, or they feel like both a girl and a boy. They are sometimes a trans boy or a trans girl, but many more are showing up who identify as nonbinary, gender fluid, genderqueer, and other gender-diverse identities. They feel like something altogether different from "boy" or "girl," or they think gender norms are just plain dumb. These children often have their own unique gender expression in terms of clothes, haircuts, and styles. And they are often frustrated that adults don't "get it" and are making such a big deal about gender identity. As one child told us, "I'm just me. What's the big deal?" Another child who identifies as nonbinary asserted, "Well, I just know I'm not a dude."

In addition to the young children arriving in our offices, we are seeing more teenagers finding, exploring, or asserting their transgender or gender diverse identities for the first time, or who are just questioning gender in general. Many of these adolescents feel the most "gender stressed," meaning that they often report higher rates of gender dysphoria, more anxiety, preoccupation, or distress related to how others treat them or how they worry others will perceive them. Often their pain is exacerbated by the appearance of secondary sex characteristics that surface when puberty unfolds, such as developing breasts, experiencing a deepening voice, or the growing of facial and body hair. These adolescents know all too well that these visible characteristics brought on by the hormonal changes of puberty result in the world even more strongly reflecting back a gender as dictated by a "girl" body or a "boy" body. Many describe painful experiences related to how others view them, dismiss their identities, or refuse to take them seriously. Some of them describe painful rejections at home, while for others, the stress comes from how they are treated at school or in the larger community. For some it is a combination of all the above.

Other children who seek our help are those who identify with their designated sex at birth (that is, they are "cisgender"), but express their gender in new and expansive ways. For example, some are cisgender boys who delight in pink sparkly shirts, leggings, or painted toenails. Others are cisgender girls who delight in their physicality, choose more masculine clothing, and enjoy playing with the boys in their class rather than the girls. These children find it ridiculous that others would question their gender just because of their clothing, hairstyles, or preferred activities. Similar to the preschoolers mentioned at the opening of this chapter, these children know that anyone can wear a dress, and clothing choice is not a reliable source of identifying gender. Children are creative and expansive in terms of how they dress and present themselves, regardless of their gender identity. They are also quite accepting of others. This will of course be influenced by how gender diversity is addressed in their families, daycare facilities, and schools, but suggests that the youngest among us are the most flexible and expansive in their thinking about gender—theirs and everyone else's.

Why Are So Many Kids Exploring Gender?

The fact that more children and teens are taking up gender identity as something to be grappled with is a reflection of the world they were born into. This world informs, reflects, and at times contradicts what children believe, know, and are learning about themselves. Today's youngest generations are growing up in a culture in which variations in gender expression are more flexible than ever, which is likely an outgrowth of the feminist movement and the various gay rights movements of the 1970s, 1980s, and 1990s, along with the more recent voices of transgender and genderqueer communities. Stores such as Target no longer divide toys based on gender. The toy giant Mattel released Creatable World in 2019, a line of six dolls that give children the opportunity to change the clothes, accessories, and hairstyles to reflect a variety of gender expressions from more feminine to more masculine. There are more gender-diverse musicians and actors than ever before, and many of them are easily recognizable due to award nominations and wins. Two trans women, Miss Netherlands and Miss Portugal, competed in the 2023 Miss Universe pageant. Examples of gender creativity in modern pop culture are seemingly endless.

Increasing numbers of colleges and universities offer gender identity options outside of male/female on forms, including some of our most elite or traditional institutions, Harvard among them. Many universities and colleges now ensure access to bathrooms aligned with gender identity and offer gender-inclusive housing, with at least one university or college doing so in all fifty states in the United States. Wellesley College, one of the oldest women's colleges in the US, has always promoted itself as a place for women who will make a difference in the world. But in March 2023, students voted on a referendum to expand the college's admissions to nonbinary and transgender students, including transgender men. No longer was it acceptable to many in the collegiate community, both faculty and students, to limit the student body to anyone who consistently identifies as a woman. As an established safe haven for people facing gender discrimination, Wellesley recognized that it was now time to keep evolving and embrace all gender minorities, especially in the face of the then-recent ramped up attacks on transgender people. The growth of gender inclusion in higher education is also happening in Canadian universities, and elite universities in Europe, such as the University of Oxford, which has clear, written policies to support increasing numbers of transgender and gender-diverse students, faculty, and staff.

In the workplace, corporate giants such as Walmart have a policy to list names and gender pronouns on employees' nametags, even if not their legal name or legal gender. The US Department of Labor's Occupational Safety and Health Administration (OSHA) states that all employers should provide transgender employees with access to bathrooms that are gender-neutral and/or align with the employee's gender identity. The state of California, going a step further, banned gender-specific single-user bathrooms in public spaces—no more waiting in line for that single toilet based on the sign on the door. Furthermore, transgender elected officials serve in governments across many nations, including in the United States, the UK Parliament, the German Federal Parliament, and Mexico's congress.

Another example of the changing gender landscape is how gender-inclusive language is becoming mainstream. The broader trend in English-speaking culture is shifting away from gendered language. For example, "mailman" is now "mail carrier," "policeman" is "police officer," and "fireman" is "firefighter." There has also been a growing body of new words to substitute for inherently gendered ones. Mx., in place of "Mr." or "Ms.," is usually pronounced like "mix" or "mux," and was first developed in the 1970s. It is more widely accepted in the United Kingdom, including on government forms, but is starting to catch on in the US.

These significant cultural shifts indicate that the increase in transgender and gender-diverse youth reflect a profound change in our cultural landscape, rather than a transitory craze. As our society becomes more accepting of transgender and gender diverse identities, and as older gender creative youth enter into adulthood, our culture and policies are changing to represent the actual fabric of our population. In turn, the evolving culture and policies create even more space for individuals to explore their gender identity and expression. We are witnessing a positive feedback loop—as the youth enter adulthood, they influence the culture, and in turn, the changed culture invites more gender expansiveness and creativity for the next generation.

And it's not just children and youth—there are also adults who have lived without conforming to gender stereotypes but didn't have language to accurately identify their gender. The cultural shift led by today's youth have allowed these adults the room to be themselves, to discover their identity in the company of many others, and it has offered language to identify their authentic gender selves more clearly. People are searching for their self to be reflected in the world, and simultaneously, we see how individuals are changing the world to reflect what is inside them.

Are Gender and Sex the Same Thing?

Sex and gender are terms that have historically been used interchangeably and were designated to a baby at birth based on external genitalia. You are a girl or you are a boy. Beginning with the rise of feminism in the 1970s, the terms "sex" and "gender" were differentiated from each other, referring to two distinct phenomena. Sex, typically male or female, was now understood to be based on the biological body, gonads, and chromosomes (XY for male and XX for female). In contrast, gender was considered to be the product of culturally created expectations of a woman and a man, social constructs known to vary across time and space. The idea that sex and gender are two separate entities, albeit intertwined, has been accepted by scholars, activists, educators, some of our legislators, and prominent professional organizations, such as the American Psychological Association (APA) and the World Health Organization (WHO). Even the United States Census Bureau holds that gender is distinct from sex, clarifying that sex refers to the biological sex of male/female, and gender refers to how an individual identifies themself. For example, a person who is DMAB would check the box "male" under the sex question. If this same person identifies as transgender, they would check the box "transgender" under the gender question or they might decide to check "female," as that is how they identify. Therefore, in a survey, a person's gender may or may not match their sex.

WHAT ABOUT SEX?

Since sex is biological, it is more straightforward and distinct, right? Not so fast. Despite the seemingly distinct categories of XY or XX chromosomes, we actually find natural variations in approximately 1.7 percent of the world's population.[1] As commonly cited, this means that the same number of people born with red hair are born with ambiguous genitalia or some variation in chromosomes, gonads, and/or sex hormones that do not fit traditional expectations of male or female bodies. These natural variations are labeled as intersex traits, some of which are observable at birth and others that are only discovered later. For example, a female baby might be born with what appears to be male genitalia and vice versa. Alternatively, some conditions are not apparent until adolescence, such as in some cases of Androgen Insensitivity Syndrome in which a genetic male is thought to be a female at birth. It is only when this child does not follow the expected puberty, such as beginning to menstruate, that further investigation reveals that they are genetically male and do not have internal female sex organs. This results from a genetic mutation in which the body is unable to use androgens, the hormones that support the development and maintenance of physically masculine characteristics. In these ways, sex has natural variations outside of the male and female boxes that society thinks of as clear and distinct.

Historically, anything outside the categories of clearly male or female at birth made people so anxious that there was felt to be no option except to "fix" it. Doctors and parents felt compelled to make a decision: Should the baby be designated female and raised as a girl, or be designated male and raised as a boy? Once that decision was made, next steps might include medical interventions such as surgery and/or socialization efforts to reinforce the child's designated gender in the midst of sex ambiguity. Unfortunately, these reassignment and socialization efforts proved to be largely unsuccessful. Some children were raised in a gender that felt wrong, and they immensely suffered from gender dysphoria and other related psychological symptoms. Others were forced to live with the physical effects of genital surgeries they were too young to consent to, such as scarring and permanent sexual dysfunction.

Eventually, driven primarily by the voices of the intersex community, all of this unnecessary suffering led to surgical intervention on intersex infants being deemed unethical unless proven medically necessary. The protocol of legislating gender assignment for intersex children has been widely condemned by many, particularly members of the intersex community who became the strongest force in alerting us to the ethical violations in these "corrective procedures" when not medically needed. Thanks to their influence, present standard practice is to let these children develop into whichever gender feels the most comfortable to them. Then medical intervention can be provided later if and when desired by the individual, when they are old enough to consent, or assent if still a child, to their own medical care. These instances of ambiguous sex are clear examples of how a baby's genitals or chromosomes at birth may not predict a child's gender. In fact, when doctors assigned a gender to intersex babies, they often got it wrong, and in many cases, no amount of medical interventions or socialization could force a child to be a gender that did not feel right to them. The lesson for all of us circles back to the basic tenet of gender we have learned: If you want to know a child's gender, listen, don't tell; that gender may or may not align with what we thought we knew from chromosomes or physiology.

WHAT EVEN IS GENDER?

Separate from sex, our understanding of gender has evolved significantly over the decades. Now we understand that gender is a complex interweaving of nature, nurture, and culture, all of which vary over time. The nature thread refers to biological aspects, such as chromosomes, gonads (primary sex characteristics), hormones, hormone receptors, secondary sex characteristics (e.g., breasts or facial hair), and the brain. People's fascination with sex differences have led to popular ideas and debates about the female brain versus the male brain or that men are from Mars and women are from Venus. You've likely heard some of the common stereotypes, such as that girls are wired to be more skilled verbally or that boys are better at spatial directions. A child's biological sex does have some impact on their physical and cerebral development starting in the womb. For example, we know from neuroscience that there are clusters of features that are more common in female brains than in male brains and vice versa. Yet, there is no such thing as an all-female brain or an all-male brain. Instead, the brain has been demonstrated to be a mosaic of traits and functions, with variations both between and within sexes.[2] Therefore, it is impossible to narrow the variations into two distinct binary categories.

The nurture thread begins even prior to birth and encompasses how a person is socialized within their family, peers, and immediate community institutions, such as school and places of worship. These threads include the ways in which we are raised, all of our life experiences, events and ordeals we are exposed to, lessons we learn over the course of our lives, and all of our social relationships. The cultural thread includes the larger values, ethics, laws, theories, and practices of a society. These threads further include beliefs, practices people share, communication, and systems of language, all of which help to determine where we fit in the world.

Finally, time is the ever-changing context in which nature, nurture, and culture interact with each other. Time captures the fact that these threads continuously vary, and therefore, gender varies over time. For example, regarding gender expressions, when I (Diane) was a little girl, I wore dresses just about every day. At the time of writing this book, many decades later, you will rarely find me in a dress, even at fancy occasions. My gender identity has remained fairly stable, but my gender expressions, how I chooses to "do" my gender, have changed dramatically over time, which leads us to ascertain a way to understand it all: "the gender web."

The Gender Web

Diane created the term "gender web" in order to capture the reality that everyone's gender is like a three-dimensional web—spun together by each and every person using the three major threads: nature, nurture, and culture.[3] Each person's gender can be thought of as a unique interweaving of these threads so that no two people's genders are exactly the same, similar to fingerprints. But unlike fingerprints that remain the same from birth to death, the gender web is neither permanent nor immutable over the course of a lifetime. That brings in the fourth dimension: time. No person's gender web can be assumed to be the same from one period of life to another, and the other threads of the web change shape with the passage of time. Therefore, the gender web may morph into different shapes or patterns. We can use the concept of the gender web as one way to understand how each of us comes to have our gender, based on our bodies, brains, and minds, and on the world around us.

Every child spins a gender web as their personal creation. While the web is certainly influenced by others, it is ultimately governed by a child's own mind, feelings, and experiences. The gender web resides within them, which they may delight in expressing for all to see, or they may hold it close as a private sense of self to be shared with only a few trusted others. Some children may hold their gender web as something that they share with no one at all, sometimes not even with themselves, if it remains buried in the less conscious layers of their psyche.

While the gender web comes with a long list of threads to keep track of, the adults must attend to all these threads if they are going to help bring a child's gender into focus. This same long list intuitively enters any parent's understanding of their own child's gender. Most importantly, it is necessary for there to be a safe and secure place to allow a child to spin their own gender web. In contrast, grabbing the threads to spin an alternative web made to adult specifications rather than a child's self-knowledge runs the risk of leaving that child all tangled up in their web, potentially damaging their confidence in themselves and in the world around them.

How Does Gender Shift Over Time?

Even if we narrow our focus on to binary male/female categories, what is considered feminine and what is considered masculine has also undergone many changes and variations over the centuries and across cultures. These changes in gender behaviors and norms are often most obvious in fashion. For example, most of us can likely remember pictures in history class of white men wearing wigs with ponytails, tights, and elaborate shirts with lace collars. If we described a person similarly attired in the present moment in the Western world, most people would likely conjure an image of a woman. Aspects of gender expression continued to evolve and change into the early twentieth century. For example, it was common to dress both boys and girls in white cotton dresses until about six years old because these garments were easy to clean and pass down to siblings. In fact, pink used to be for boys, and blue was for girls. The idea of separating baby clothing by gender or color didn't appear until 1918 when a department store trade publication declared *pink for boys* and *blue for girls*. This remained true until the 1940s when department stores in the United States switched the colors based on what retailers thought families preferred—pink for girls, blue for boys.[4] This broadly accepted reversal in gender norms for pink and blue was not based on a discovery of essential sex-typed color-coding, but rather the result of marketing to sell more clothes and increase profits!

In addition to gender changes within a culture or across cultures, each person experiences their own intrapersonal gender shifts over the course of their lifetime. We might see clear examples of these internal shifts when a person comes out as a different gender from the one designated to them at birth or when a person's gender identity shifts more than once. For example, a child designated female at birth may initially come out as a trans boy as they are locating their gender as more masculine. Then over time, this same child might choose a different term to describe themselves, such as nonbinary because this descriptor feels like a better fit for all the masculine and feminine parts of themselves.

We see gender shifts happen within all of us over the course of our lifetimes, no matter if we are cisgender or transgender or some other gender. For example, a young male athlete may feel pressured to be tough, restricting him to feel and express more stereotypically masculine traits. This young man may grow up and find himself caring less about what others think. Maybe after becoming a parent, he'll experience himself connecting with more stereotypically feminine traits, like nurturing and caretaking. Before fatherhood, those traits may have lain dormant, suppressed, or perhaps were never on his radar, but then later became a significant part of his gender self.

Just as a person's internal gender identity, gender expressions, and relationship to gender are likely to evolve over time, so does gender in our culture, which in turn affects shifts in our gender sensibilities about ourselves. These shifts do not mean that an earlier stage was wrong or mistaken. Instead, each change in our experience of our own gender is a necessary step in locating an evolving and growing self in a changing world. And even though an individual's internal sense of who they are changes over time, as it does for all of us, no one can be made to change their internal sense of self by someone else, even if they are forced to conform outwardly to social norms. We see proof of this in all the gender-diverse people who are out as their authentic selves in spite of the extreme public pressure to conform. We also observe it in those who wrap themselves in a cloak of invisibility—where they are "in" rather than "out" about their gender—but still claim their authentic gender for themselves, allowing no one to deny them of it, even if they don't publicly display it.

Beyond Gender Norms

Despite all the gender variations and changes, gender (like sex) has historically been divided into binary categories of "man" or "woman" in Western culture. This either/or thinking pushed the two genders to be experienced and reinforced as opposites to each other with no options outside the categories.

Historically, boys were taught to be the strong and ambitious gender and were allowed to engage in rough-and-tumble play. They were encouraged to be logical and assertive men who pursued a variety of jobs or careers. If they failed to live up to their masculine gender, they were disparagingly called names such as "sissy" or "girly." This pejorative referencing as "female" simultaneously served as a devaluation of girls as the weak and passive gender—crybabies, overly emotional, timid, preferring dolls over darts. Girls were taught to be mothers and help-mates, while boys were construed as destined to conquer the world, if given class access to that destiny. If not, they could at least dominate their households.

These gender norms of the dominant culture reinforced the standards for what constituted a proper woman or a proper man. Once parents and medical providers determined you were male or female at birth, the path was set—you were now a boy or a girl respectively, not just now, but forever. Today's children and youth, however, are not having this. They are challenging the limits and negative connotations of these mutually exclusive gender boxes and, in many cases, are stepping outside the boxes completely. Despite the enthusiasm of younger generations, many adults see this breakdown of the gender binary as a threat to society. When I (Diane) was growing up, with the advent of rock 'n' roll, the Beatles, and the youth movements that followed, it was common to talk about the generation gap. The way of this generation was seen as a threat to the way of those who came before. We are now witnessing a new generation gap as young people's celebration of the breakdown of binary gender clashes with their elders' fear of losing that very social order.

The Gender Movers and Shakers

This recent explosion in youth living outside the stereotypical boy/girl boxes is not a new or foreign phenomenon. Looking back on the twentieth century, we find decades of youth challenging the strict binary nature of gender and the rules surrounding it. By 1920, activists succeeded in securing voting rights for women after more than seventy years of convening, protests, hunger strikes, and imprisonment. Then came the roaring twenties, and the rise of fashion and behaviors that directly and further challenged gender norms. Young women began cutting their hair, smoking, and wearing shorter skirts and box-fit dresses. Some demanded the same sexual freedom previously accorded only to men. Consequently, they were criticized for being immoral and androgynous because of their gender nonconforming behaviors and expressions. As we know now, these new ways of being a woman turned out to not be a dangerous trend or a passing fad. Instead, the 1920s became the opportunity for women's social behaviors and fashion to become more androgynous or masculine in the subsequent decades. We saw this fashion shift further unfold in trousers, pants suits, and blue jeans.

It was not just what women wore or how they acted in private. Social roles shifted. Women not previously in the workforce took over men's jobs during World War II and many refused to go home after the war, even when castigated for being "un-American." Obviously, their lack of patriotism was not really the issue. They had readily served their country when called upon. Instead, it was about making room for the men returning from war to restore their peacetime role as breadwinner, with woman back at the hearth. Reflecting back, these young women's challenges to traditional gender norms became the phenomenon critics sought to squash. Yet, the effort failed as we witnessed women increasingly pursue jobs traditionally reserved for men, even in the face of gender discrimination that exists to this day.

As social norms changed and the box for what is acceptable for women continued to expand, the box for men began to widen, too. We saw this in the 1960s when young men started growing their hair long, adorning themselves with beads and necklaces, wearing tie-dyed shirts and embroidered jeans. As the decades continued, men's social roles became less rigid as they took on more parenting responsibilities or chose careers previously reserved for women, such as nursing, nannying, or early childhood education. Then gay rights movements followed by the more inclusive LGBTQ+ social movements were all in full force by the end of the twentieth century, all vital contributors to the expansion of the gender boxes beyond the binary.

At each of these turning points, young people involved in these "gender revolutions" were accused of either immoral behavior or engaging in a passing fad. To the contrary, youth were setting great change into motion. While the two gender boxes had worked for many people, they had created suffering for numerous others. Think of the little girl made to believe that her intelligence and dreams didn't matter, since she would become only a mother, never a doctor. Or think of the adolescent boy battling depression, who suffered alone because he was a gentle soul who was supposed to be tough.

From where we stand—two psychologists from different generations—we witness and personally experience that we all benefit as the boxes for male and female expand. Fathers are able to take family leave and be more involved in their children's upbringing. Mental health for both genders is being openly talked about. There is more space for boys and men to express vulnerable emotions and more space for girls and women to assert themselves with no aspersion on their character. By the time we arrived in the twenty-first century, all of these shifts toward more flexible gender expressions rocked and cracked the foundation of sex and gender that had been laid down by previous generations—the one that strictly placed and then policed gender in one of two boxes, boy/girl, man/woman.

Thinking and Being Beyond Boxes

Despite all these changes and increased flexibility for the male and female genders, the gender boxes remain. Some children look out into the world and see the remaining constraints on girl/woman and boy/man. Some of these children do not fit within these constraints; they simply cannot locate themselves in the boxes offered by society. There is a long history of people who have identified with the opposite gender, who today we might refer to as a trans woman or a trans man. Until relatively recently, however, there was never space or attention given to anything in between or outside binary genders. There was only binary box-jumping: a woman discovered they were a man, or a man discovered they were a woman. This binary thinking leaves little room for all the ambiguity, nuance, and gray areas that make up a human life and any individual's unique gender web, but it's common in our society. Something is right or wrong, true or false, acceptable or unacceptable. Perhaps we have had a natural tendency toward binary thinking in our culture because it's so useful in promoting quick thinking, decision making, and sorting information. Our culture overvalues all three of these qualities.

Fortunately, human minds are creative and complex, so binary thinking is not the only way. Compare it to "full-spectrum thinking," a way of exercising our minds to consider possibilities outside of defined boxes, or operating between two boxes, or existing without boxes, and so on.[5] Full-spectrum thinking opens up the space to look at the reality of a human life in all its messiness, nuance, and shades of gray.

We have all likely encountered situations and ideas that are impossible to accurately fit into categories or to place ourselves in one of two boxes. For example, we could ask, "Are you a cat person or a dog person?" Many people will be able to answer this question immediately with a resounding "cat" or "dog." They might also be able to tell you immediately if their spouse or child is a cat or dog person. Maybe you are one of these people. But what if instead you like *both* cats *and* dogs? Or maybe you like *neither* cats *nor* dogs, or maybe you are neutral about cats and dogs, but have a strong preference for bunnies, and so on. While this is a whimsical example, we can see how quickly the thinking can become complicated if we replace cat and dog with concepts of male and female or masculine and feminine. The possibilities can be endless.

When someone attempts to locate themselves outside the boy/man and girl/woman boxes, it requires a lot more exploration and cognitive energy. It requires creativity and experimentation. Full-spectrum thinking requires the capacity to sit in ambiguity and a state of not knowing because there are few preexisting and clearly defined boundaries. This can be quite difficult and anxiety-provoking as it goes against our need for certainty. No wonder the default has been the binary!

Full-Spectrum Thinking Among Youth Today

While our society tends to think in duality or either/or terms, younger generations are becoming full-spectrum thinkers, going beyond the binary, and thinking outside the box. Even though boy or girl are still options, many children and youth today are finding masculinity and femininity to be on a continuum rather than as two distinct boxes. Furthermore, some children and youth are locating themselves completely outside the binary, as they apply full-spectrum thinking to their own gender and those around them. Recall the young person who reflected on their own gender with, "Well, I know I'm not a dude." Here is full-spectrum thinking on full display. Designated male at birth, this youth knows for now that "dude" is not a good fit, but they are still in the realm of exploration of what will eventually be the gender "fit" for them. In the meantime, they are able to suspend themselves in a state of not yet knowing, but thinking about it—their gender, that is. These young people no longer experience gender as a given aspect of one's self that is fixed at birth. Instead, gender is an aspect of identity to be explored, discovered, and created similar to other aspects of identity that adolescents have grappled with for decades, like their racial or ethnic identity, their political stance, or their future role in society.

This exploration of gender as an aspect of identity is one that many young people are taking up regardless of their gender identity—cisgender or not. Even if they resonate with the sex designated to them at birth, children and youth today are less likely to make assumptions about the gender identity of their peers and are more likely to be accepting of a variety of gender identities. Gender is no longer a given, predetermined by the sex designated at birth. You might say it's up for grabs and requires exploration and reflection on yourself and on your gender. This is what I (Diane) termed "gender creativity."[6]

These significant cultural shifts alert us that the explosion of youth identifying as transgender, nonbinary, or gender expansive, or challenging the social rules of gender, is not a passing fad or dangerous trend that suddenly popped up a few years ago, driven by social media and the internet. Instead, it is the outgrowth of the gender evolution evident in the twentieth century. Gender creative youth are leading the way to expansive identity options that cannot be contained in a box, such as bigender, genderqueer, agender, demiboy, demigirl, and many others. Once you step outside the binary, the space opens to reflect on who you are, on gender and how you relate to it, suggesting infinite combinations and variations. As we watch this phenomenon unfold, we are learning that in order for children and youth to *explore* who they are, they have to be given the space to *be* who they are.

Scholars and practitioners of previous generations talked the talk—critiquing and challenging the gender binary, calling for more expansive gender identities and expressions. But today's youth are actually walking the walk—*living* outside the binary and pushing for constantly expanding perimeters of gender. As we have seen, cultural shifts have made space for young people to reject binary gender boxes and create new models of gender. The bedrock of gender norms in our society is shifting, and youth are taking this opportunity to develop their own ideas and norms about it—both how you do gender and how you be it. The youth are not only rocking this foundation but also moving heavy boulders, and this involves some heavy lifting.

As the youth lead the way, they open up the space for all of us to examine our own unique gender journeys; how our identities have changed and will continue to change over the course of our lives. Today's youth are showing us that gender identity can be unique and individual. Our children are teaching us well. What a world it would be if more of us, not just the children, could take the time to engage in full-spectrum thinking. We'd have the opportunity to reflect, not just on our gender, but on our whole selves—asking what drives us to act, present ourselves, or interact with others the way we do. If adults can engage with full-spectrum thinking, we, along with the children, will have the opportunity to contribute to a more caring and compassionate society that makes room for people across the gender spectrum.

CHAPTER 3

Why Does Gender Make People So Anxious?

When we are no longer able to change a situation,
we are challenged to change ourselves.
— Viktor Frankl (Austrian psychiatrist)

IF GENDER AND GENDER NORMS HAVE ALWAYS shifted over time, and if the current changes might offer benefits to our society, why are adults so anxious in the midst of gender expansiveness and shifting gender norms? Our world is rapidly changing, challenging all of us to shift and adapt faster and faster. This is most obvious with technological advances. Let's take the example of one invention—the smartphone. The smartphone changed so much in terms of how we consume and share information, how we connect and relate with each other, how much we are expected to be available to others, and even how we spend our free time. Youth, in particular, are spending more time in structured activities and on their smartphones to stay connected with their peers, while having less time in the real world with friends. Adults look on with humor, confusion, and even concern, when teenagers, finally meeting up in person, stay on their devices while sitting right next to each other. In response to this technology and the changing social structures, a simple Google search will turn up many research projects, articles, and op-eds attempting to grapple with questions such as, "Is the smart phone leading to the mental health problems in youth? Does screen time have negative impacts on brain and social development? What does this mean for the future of society?" And all this anxiety is in reaction to one device that most of us carry nearly everywhere. Change creates anxiety!

This simplified example demonstrates how old social structures, values, and ways of doing things are being broken down, sending individuals and entire communities into a state of anxiety—insecure about the future of humankind and shaken by a perceived loss of control. Regardless, social changes in our world are underway for better or for worse, and there is no stopping the forward momentum. The only real control any person or community can have is how we respond to changes, and how we direct our forward movement—whether with thoughtfulness and support or with fear and reactivity. This is also true in the midst of changing gender norms.

The Brain On Change

The seemingly rapid changes in gender norms and gender diversity create immense anxiety, particularly in adults, even though these changes aren't new. Gender changes are not incorporated as seamlessly as a smartphone, since they are directly shifting the very foundation of our social order. People don't understand what is going on as they experience these seismic shifts in gender, and the unknown feels threatening. Even though our human lives are full of change, our tendency is to respond to rapid or massive changes with initial resistance and unease. Any kind of change, even desired ones such as starting a new job, tend to make humans feel anxious, ungrounded, and unsettled as our brains go into high alert, scanning the environment for errors and danger. Fortunately, our brains are also flexible, which allows us to learn new things and adapt to changing circumstances throughout our lifetimes. Given how much change can stress our nervous systems, we are lucky that our brains are so adaptable!

Generally, humans much prefer the familiar and predictable because it makes us feel safe and secure, and our brains use much less energy when things feel continuous, permanent, and/or routine. A common understanding of how we process information is referred to as the Dual Processing Theory, meaning that our brains contain two processing systems—System 1 (fast thinking) and System 2 (slow thinking). Fast thinking is automatic, unconscious, unintentional, uncontrollable, biased, and generates immediate impressions and feelings. These can then become persistent beliefs and attitudes if endorsed by System 2. The slow thinking of System 2 is the conscious, rational, analytical processes in our brains. This is our general intelligence, which requires much more effort and is much slower than System 1. Daniel Kahneman, who popularized these ideas in his book *Thinking, Fast and Slow*, notes that people tend to place too much faith in their intuition and avoid cognitive effort as much as possible.[1] Perhaps a more generous explanation is that our brains are designed to conserve energy and therefore use fast thinking whenever possible. The capacity to conserve energy is important because our brains consume 20 to 25 percent of it, but even more shocking, young children's brains consume upward of 60 percent of the body's energy![2]

Dual processing theory is a helpful way to conceptualize how we think about gender, which is one of those things that people throughout the world and throughout history have often experienced as obvious and permanent. Gender was a given that did not require any exploration, the patterns of gender were more or less predictable, and entire social structures developed around it. Perhaps because of the experience of gender as a fixed cornerstone of our world, the human brain often uses our fast-thinking system to sort new people into genders so quickly and automatically that we're not even consciously aware of the power of gender as an organizing principle. Gender may rise to consciousness only when we are shocked out of our fast, automatic thinking by encountering someone who our brains cannot quickly and accurately place in a gender box. The unease this can create gives rise to a variety of feelings and actions depending on the individual. You might find yourself in a state of curiosity, confusion, anxiety, anger, and/or even disgust when jolted out of autopilot. When forced into slow thinking (System 2), you might even feel an urgency to know what gender this person is, what their sex is, what their body is like, and even what is between their legs. Most importantly, if we don't slow down and use our logical minds to pay attention to our negative feelings and reactions about someone's gender, our automatic response is to avoid, ignore, or silence the experience that made us feel uncomfortable.

Nobody likes feeling uncomfortable. The resulting lack of processed emotions and reactions become fertile ground for the creation and perpetuation of myths and misinformation about gender diversity. You may have had the experience of heading down an aisle in a grocery store, approaching someone pushing their cart in your direction who is wearing a dress and sporting a bushy beard. If you had time to reflect, you might come up with several different thoughts about this person: Maybe it's a man who likes dresses or someone who knows themself to be a woman but accepted the body changes that came with their puberty and that's the way they live their gender. But with no time to think, an immediate reflexive rather than reflective response might be: "Weird." As mentioned earlier, our automatic feelings and impressions can become beliefs and attitudes if not rejected by our System 2 processing. We can allow our feelings of discomfort to be used as evidence that something is wrong with the object of our discomfort (i.e., transgender and gender-diverse people). These feelings of discomfort can be further fueled by voices, both inner and outer, telling us that being transgender is not real; transgender people are mentally ill; gender-diverse youth are being groomed by malevolent people or just doing it to get attention or be part of the in-group; gender identity is contagious; and youth, particularly girls, are susceptible to social influencers. No wonder there is so much anxiety and misunderstanding surrounding gender-affirmative care!

Given humans' resistance to change and the fact that gender has generally been considered a foundation of human civilization, it is understandable that rapidly changing gender norms create a lot of anxiety. It feels contradictory to all the socialization that adults receive about gender and culture throughout their lives. This type of change requires more brain power as we attempt to reorient ourselves. It means we have to tolerate a state of not knowing—not knowing what a particular person's gender is, not knowing the new gender norms and possibilities beyond two boxes, and sometimes not knowing the right language to use. We might find ourselves feeling even less certain if we can still label ourselves as belonging to only one box or wondering more about our own gender identity. Despite the inherent challenges in accommodating big transitions, change has always been an inevitable part of living a human life and an essential component of both societal and personal creativity. This is also how changing gender norms gives rise to gender creativity. Now we just need to put our minds to work and use our collective creativity to ensure a safe and compassionate world for people of all genders.

Seeking Information to Find Security

When people feel anxious and confused they tend to seek out further information, often looking to experts for reassurance and direction. I (Michelle) sometimes search my health symptoms on Google when feeling anxious, even though I already know that the answers are going to range from "It's nothing" to "It's a brain tumor." I rationally know there is no way to accurately diagnose myself through a search on Google. It doesn't help my anxiety, and in many cases, it makes my anxiety worse because I am more likely to focus on the serious diagnosis rather than feel reassured by the simplest explanation. But sometimes, I do it anyway, hoping the information will give me a feeling of security.

In fact, it is well documented in research that anxious people tend to hyperfocus on information that feels threatening, and they tend to overlook or minimize the information that is more neutral or positive. The human brain prioritizes threatening information, which makes sense because the recognition of threats can be lifesaving. In fact, this feature of the brain likely helped our ancestors survive in a very different world. Unfortunately, this continued focus on threatening information in modern society often makes anxious people unnecessarily more anxious. Yet, accessing accurate and helpful information can help us decide what to do.

In the case of children and gender, the experts with accurate information are those with training and experience in pediatric gender care. These experts provide direct care to transgender and gender-diverse children, youth, and their families. Pediatric gender specialists conduct, write, and stay current on the latest research. They consult and learn from each other all over the world. Diane and I have certainly learned a lot over the past decades as the field of pediatric gender care has grown. Consequently, there is more research than ever that demonstrates that the most effective ways of treating gender dysphoria and supporting transgender and gender-diverse children and teens is through gender-affirming care and family support.

Gender-affirming care is an interdisciplinary approach to support children and youth in their gender identity as opposed to trying to force them to dress or act in a way that is deemed "correct" for their designated sex. It will be examined more closely in the following chapter, but for now, gender-affirming care is a large umbrella term that can include social transition, mental health therapy, puberty blockers, hormone treatment, surgical interventions, and consultation with families, schools, and medical centers. If you're feeling anxious about your child's gender identity, these experts in pediatric gender care can answer your questions and help you to feel more secure.

What Is Gender Dysphoria?

A person might feel distress when their own gender identity (who they feel they are) is different from their designated sex (based on their chromosomes and genitalia) at birth. This feeling is called gender dysphoria. The standard diagnostic manual for mental health disorders, which is called the *Diagnostic and Statistical Manual of Mental Disorders* (DSM-5-TR), provides an overarching diagnosis of gender dysphoria with separate specific criteria for children and for adolescents and adults. The DSM-5-TR defines gender dysphoria in adolescents and adults as: "a significant difference between one's experienced/expressed gender and their designated gender, lasting at least six months, as manifested by at least two of the following.

- A marked incongruence between one's experienced/expressed gender and primary and/or secondary sex characteristics (or in young adolescents, the anticipated secondary sex characteristics).

- A strong desire to be rid of one's primary and/or secondary sex characteristics because of a marked incongruence with one's experienced/expressed gender (or in young adolescents, a desire to prevent the development of the anticipated secondary sex characteristics).

- A strong desire for the primary and/or secondary sex characteristics of the other gender.

- A strong desire to be of the other gender (or some alternative gender different from one's assigned gender).

- A strong desire to be treated as the other gender (or some alternative gender different from one's assigned gender).

- A strong conviction that one has the typical feelings and reactions of the other gender (or some alternative gender different from one's assigned gender)."

When it comes to children, the DSM-5-TR defines gender dysphoria as: "a marked incongruence between one's experienced/expressed gender and their assigned gender, lasting at least six months, as manifested by at least six of the following (one of which must be the first criterion).

- A strong desire to be of the other gender or an insistence that one is the other gender (or some alternative gender different from one's assigned gender).

- In boys (assigned gender), a strong preference for cross-dressing or simulating female attire; or in girls (assigned gender), a strong preference for wearing only typical masculine clothing and a strong resistance to the wearing of typical feminine clothing.

- A strong preference for cross-gender roles in make-believe play or fantasy play.

- A strong preference for the toys, games, or activities stereotypically used or engaged in by the other gender.

- A strong preference for playmates of the other gender.

- In boys (assigned gender), a strong rejection of typically masculine toys, games, and activities and a strong avoidance of rough-and-tumble play; or in girls (assigned gender), a strong rejection of typically feminine toys, games, and activities.

- A strong dislike of one's sexual anatomy.

- A strong desire for the physical sex characteristics that match one's experienced gender."[3]

With the diagnostic criteria both for adolescents/adults and for children, gender dysphoria must also be associated with significant distress or impairment in social, occupational, or other important areas of functioning. While these are the most current criteria as of the writing of this book, one can see how the criteria are already outdated by focusing on binary girl/boy genders and do not adequately capture the diverse gender identities that we see in our practices. Nonbinary and other gender-diverse youth also contend with gender dysphoria.

If not treated properly, gender dysphoria can result in debilitating anxiety, depression, and self-harm, and is associated with higher rates of suicide. A national survey by the Trevor Project, a nonprofit organization that supports LGBTQ+ youth, found in 2020 that 60 percent of trans teens and young adults reported engaging in self-harm during the preceding twelve months, and over 75 percent reported symptoms of generalized anxiety disorder in the preceding two weeks.[4] The Trevor Project's national survey in 2021 found that 52 percent of transgender and nonbinary youth reported seriously considering suicide in the previous year with 20 percent having made a suicide attempt.[5] Proper treatment for gender dysphoria is "gender-affirming care" as per state, country, and international professional organizations, such as the World Professional Association for Transgender Health (WPATH). Pediatric gender-affirming care is aimed at supporting a child and their family as they explore their identity with no pressure to be *any* particular gender.

While the distress of transgender and gender-diverse youth is often talked about as being rooted in gender dysphoria, it is important to note that not all of these youth experience gender dysphoria as described above. Many youths describe that while they are comfortable with their bodies, instead, their dysphoria is rooted in how their physical traits out them to others as transgender or nonbinary or how these traits encourage others to misgender them. Additionally, gender expressions that appear to not fit with someone's secondary sex characteristics tend to cause negativity or criticism from others, creating the basis for gender dysphoria. Instead, their desire to make their appearance conform to a particular gender is often in response to the social pressure to comply with more stereotypical gender expressions.

What Does Gender Dysphoria Feel Like?

One nonbinary youth, twenty years old, described gender dysphoria this way: "Sometimes it's my voice, other times it's my body itself. It's the feeling of being trapped and imprisoned in something you didn't choose and did nothing to deserve. It's reinforced every time I get misgendered."[6]

If you have never experienced gender dysphoria, we invite you to try out a little experiment. It is important to note that the real lived experience of gender dysphoria is highly individual and personal and cannot be fully captured here. Imagine that tomorrow morning you wake up and things don't feel right. Maybe you have breasts where there had been none, maybe your genitals are completely wrong, or maybe there is nothing different about your body, but something feels strange. Now, imagine you sit at the breakfast table and your family or housemate are referring to you as a different pronoun than what you have always used; they refer to this body you're in by calling you "He" in the place of "She" or vice versa. You tell them they are mistaken, and they look at you with confusion and concern. You try to explain that they are wrong about your gender, or perhaps clarify that you woke up in the wrong body. Perhaps their concerned looks begin to suggest they think you're crazy, even as they attempt to be supportive. On the way to work, you notice people stare at you on the subway, the barista at the coffee shop refers to you as "sir" or "ma'am," again referencing the wrong gender. Everyone at work also misgenders you. You go into whichever bathroom matches your gender, or perhaps you find that neither the men's nor the women's restrooms match your gender, so you end up just picking one. Imagine that people in the bathroom give you a weird look, or someone even tells you to get out because you are in the wrong bathroom. No matter how often you correct people, the misgendering never stops. By this point, you might be feeling crazy. You are spending a lot of time and energy trying to figure out how to correct this misperception of you. You constantly wonder: Do I need to tell everyone my correct pronouns? How do I help people see me as I see myself? Maybe if I cut my hair differently, or wore different clothes, or maybe if I changed my name to a more masculine or more feminine name people would stop seeing and referring to me as a gender that I am not? How will I ever be able to just go about my day without always having to be reminded of gender and my own gender identity that is not recognized? If I can't fix this, how am I ever going to feel comfortable living in this world? We have invited you to engage in this experiment in order to demonstrate the importance of trying to imagine the experience of transgender and gender-diverse people. This is important because cisgender people often cannot or do not imagine what this is like, and it is through empathy that we can begin to understand experiences outside of our own.

This experiment hopefully conveys two points. First, that you continued to feel like the gender you know yourself to be despite the imagined changes to your body, how others looked at you, or how they referred to you. No one could convince you that you are this other gender. Similarly, transgender and gender-diverse people cannot be convinced to be any other gender, no matter how painful their daily experience. Second, the experience of being misgendered is distressing, and it happens countless times throughout the day. Consequently, a transgender or gender-diverse person may frequently be distracted from attending to what is in front of them, because instead of focusing on work or school, transgender and gender-diverse children and youth have to spend excessive mental and emotional energy on the simplest interactions with others, including the navigation of bathrooms. Additionally, these youth are distressed by how others see them on top of the already normal self-consciousness of adolescence. They may also worry about being socially isolated or even bullied at school. All these additional experiences and concerns that a gender-diverse youth contends with are what is referred to as "gender noise." This noise is typically generated from the external environment, which is persistently stressing the internal world of an individual. Sometimes it is a constant hum in the background, and at other times, it is experienced as loud and significantly disruptive. Now add on all the complications of sexuality and dating, and imagine how all of this impacts both school performance and social interactions in a young transgender or gender-diverse person! So, how do we help children and youth with the distress of gender dysphoria?

Treatment of Gender Dysphoria

Gender-affirming medical care for youth includes access to puberty blockers (medication that pauses the progression of puberty temporarily) and hormones (i.e., estrogen or testosterone) for those who meet specific criteria. The use of puberty blockers and hormones is evidence-based, meaning that research studies consistently demonstrate that the mental health of transgender and gender-diverse youth greatly improves with access to gender-affirming medical care. Youth who access puberty blockers and/or gender-affirming hormone treatment present with significantly decreased depression and suicidality, and improved self-esteem, body image, and quality of life. Various research studies have found the following.

- Approximately nine in ten trans adults who wanted but did not receive puberty-blocking treatment reported *lifetime* suicidal ideation.[7]

- The use of puberty blockers during adolescence is associated with significantly lower *lifetime* suicidal ideation compared to those who desired blockers but did not receive them.[8]

- After an average of two years on puberty blockers, the percentage of youth who had been experiencing behavioral problems dropped from 44 to 22 percent.[9]

- After an average of two years on puberty blockers, the percentage of those experiencing emotional problems dropped from 30 to 10 percent.[10]

- A 40 percent decrease in depression and suicidality occurred when puberty blockers and gender-affirming hormones were prescribed to transgender youth who wanted and qualified for the treatment.[11]

- Large improvements in psychological well-being were documented soon after beginning gender-affirming hormone therapy (GAHT).[12]

- A 75 percent reduction in the level of suicidality in adolescents occurred after one year of hormone treatment.[13]

- A survey of 11,914 transgender and nonbinary youth found that the use of gender-affirming hormone treatment among those ages thirteen to seventeen was associated with nearly 40 percent lower odds of recent depression and attempting suicide in the past year compared to youth who wanted but could not access hormone treatment.[14]

- Transgender adults who accessed gender-affirming hormone therapy during ages thirteen to seventeen had a 135 percent decrease in adjusted odds for past-year suicidal ideation when compared to those who wanted hormones but never had access to them.[15]

• Transgender adults who had access to gender-affirming hormones in late adolescence had a 62 percent decrease in adjusted odds for past-year suicidal ideation, and those who accessed GAHT only in adulthood had a 21 percent decrease in past-year suicidal ideation compared to adults who wanted hormones but never had access to them. This indicates that access to GAHT in early adolescence has the most significant impact on lower suicidality in adulthood.[16]

Despite the availability of significant research that demonstrates the efficacy of gender-affirming medical care, the media frequently report on it without reference to this research. Additionally, the media neglect to disclose the grave consequences when youth are denied access to care. Unfortunately, the media often give a platform to uninformed commentators and self-appointed "experts" with no actual knowledge or experience in pediatric gender care. These voices produce sensational headlines that induce fear and drown out the voices of actual pediatric gender care experts. When gender-affirming providers are included, mainstream media often take their words out of context. For example, a pediatric gender specialist might say, "It is important to follow a child's lead when working to understand their gender identity." Yet, media reports may misconstrue this statement as advocating that everyone must do whatever a child says. Other misconceptions include if an adolescent wants puberty blockers, just hand them over; if they want hormones or surgery, no problem. To the contrary, there are specific criteria that an adolescent must meet in order to qualify for any of these medical interventions. Additionally, there are significant barriers for many families to find care, such as limited access to gender-affirming providers due to location, long waiting lists, and in certain cases, financial constraints that make pursuing care impossible. Unfortunately, however, in an age of electronic communications, information travels with such lightning speed that even false information spreads around the world in a moment.

Misinformation in the Media

In addition to the research that is omitted in the media, misinformation regarding gender-affirming care abounds. Misinformation is information that is factually incorrect, and it can come from anywhere. Remember the childhood game of Telephone? The information is accurate as reported, but in the repeated retelling of it, the information becomes distorted. Or maybe there was an error in the newscast or someone simply misremembered the information. Perhaps a person repeats something they've heard, but unbeknownst to them, the information is untrue. One example of this kind of misinformation is when people make generalized statements that are not based on facts. Someone says, "My friend's child says she's transgender, and I think it is just a phase. Kids are just doing whatever their friends are doing, and these days teens think it's cool to be transgender." The second statement about a cool fad is a generalization that is not based on facts and has no bearing on the truth of the first statement—a child who says she's transgender.

Similar to misinformation, disinformation is a term used to capture false information. Unlike misinformation, disinformation has a malicious intent. It is spread for the purpose of misleading and manipulating people and/or influencing public opinion in some way. An example of disinformation in the media includes reports on false statistics that suggest high rates of regret after gender-affirming medical care, when in fact these procedures tend to have unusually low rates of regret. This disinformation is likely spread in an attempt to discredit gender-affirming providers rather than to educate the public. We witness both misinformation and disinformation when it comes to transgender issues, and no more strongly than in media coverage of gender diversity in children and youth. It creates further confusion and raises anxiety levels even higher than they would be otherwise. This is happening in the media, both liberal left-leaning and conservative right-leaning, throughout the United States and other Western countries.

For example, *The New York Times* has faced criticism for biased reporting in its articles on transgender people. Some of these have even appeared on the front page with an accompanying three-page spread, specifically focusing on gender-affirming medical treatments involving children and youth. *The New York Times* has been accused of holding a negative bias in their reporting, particularly given that their articles have been used in court-rulings to support anti-transgender legislation. In response, hundreds of current and former contributors to the paper, and thousands of subscribers, including both of us, signed letters to *The New York Times* editorial board protesting that their coverage of transgender people violated its editorial guidelines.

The allegations of bias especially pertain to the *Times* presenting gender-affirming medical treatments for youth as though they are not evidence-based and supported by scientific research demonstrating the effectiveness of these treatments. One particular article reported on the allegations of Jamie Reed, a former staffer at the Transgender Center at St. Louis Children's Hospital.[17] Reed made many claims such as that the clinic prescribed puberty blockers that had caused liver toxicity in a child and that the family had written an angry email to the clinic. This family, who had previously remained private, even spoke to the *Times*'s journalist in order to get the truth out to the public. The family provided evidence that documented there was no clear link between their child's liver trouble and puberty blockers. The family also provided the actual email they had sent to the clinic, clearly showing that it was misconstrued by Reed. This evidence proved that Reed's allegations were false, and the family spoke out because they wanted the world to know how the clinic had saved their child's life. Several additional parents of children treated at the clinic spoke with the same journalist because they also wanted to show that Reed's allegations were indeed false, and that the gender-affirming clinic had provided their children with excellent health care. Finally, an internal investigation also found Reed's allegations to be unsubstantiated. Yet, the article portrayed Reed and her allegations as just as accurate as the parents who were defending the clinic.[18]

On the other end of the political spectrum in the United States, Fox News also reports on gender-affirming medical care for children and youth. In one example, their news anchor reported that gender-affirming medical providers were giving *hormones* to five-year-olds. If this were true, it would mean that five-year-olds would be walking around with breasts, deeper voices, acne, and all the other signs of puberty. Appalling! If you actually believed this, one might imagine that you would be horrified and tell everyone you see about this atrocity. "Can you believe it?" If you were to bring this to us, we would know that you were getting your information from poor sources. We would help you understand that this is not true, hormones are not available to prepubescent children, and are available only to some adolescents who meet specific criteria. Now, which one evokes more emotion: "hormones to five-year-olds" or "no, not true"? Which one is easier to remember? Which one makes for a good story? That which evokes emotion is much more memorable and certainly makes for a more exciting story to sell.

Once incorrect information is out in the mainstream it is very hard to correct public opinion or perception after widespread reporting, regardless of the topic. For example, at the start of the COVID-19 pandemic, some media misreported on the possible use or ingestion of household disinfectants as potentially preventing and/or treating disease. Despite this claim being false, the calls to poison control increased significantly as a result of people turning to household disinfectants. In response, the Centers for Disease Control and Prevention (CDC) conducted a survey of 502 adults and found that 39 percent were engaging in unsafe practices such as washing food with bleach, applying household cleaners directly to skin, and inhaling or ingesting disinfectants in an attempt to prevent COVID-19 infections because they had believed the misinformation that had circulated.[19] Much time and energy was then put into trying to correct the misinformation in order to keep people from harm. Regretfully, we have no comparable government Center for Gender Health agency to oversee, monitor, or control the dire consequences of the dissemination of gender mis- and disinformation.

Legislating Gender

Transgender rights have improved throughout many areas of the world, but simultaneously, sexuality and gender rights have also been politically targeted in countries such as Brazil, Poland, the United Kingdom, and here in the United States. Gender legislation demonstrates an apparent sociocultural anxiety and it appears to be rising around the globe, as proven by changes in legislation in regard to transgender children and youth. In the United States, 174 transgender-related bills were introduced in 2022, of which twenty-six passed.[20] The following year, over 550 anti-trans bills were introduced,[21] in response to which twenty of the fifty states passed laws or policies that either ban gender-affirming care or limit access to gender-affirming medical care for youth. This includes some states, such as South Carolina, that banned gender-affirming care for transgender and gender-diverse people up to age twenty-six.[22] In addition, some of these bills aim to regulate the school curriculum in order to ban discussions of gender or sexuality, take away the privacy of trans youth in their school settings under the guise of parental rights, bar transgender children from sports, and even ban drag shows that could possibly be viewed by those under eighteen years old.

The rhetoric behind these bills is that children and youth are in danger of being coerced into a transgender identity and into medical interventions that they will later regret. In essence, these bills would have you believe that we need to save the children, preserve their innocence, and protect them from the LGBTQ+ community and from gender-affirming professionals who are invested in influencing young people to embrace an inauthentic transgender or gender-diverse identity. These bills also threaten parental rights for making health care decisions for their children and, in some cases, forbid them from accessing the evidence-based care for treating gender dysphoria.

Given that change-anxiety can drive faulty thinking, it becomes easy to recognize that this legislation is not about saving children. Instead, it is a social manifestation of anxiety and the desperate need to point a finger at an identifiable cause of fear, so that attempts can be made to get rid of the so-called danger. It is an exploitation of fear for political ends. Rather than saving children, the legislation has already—and will continue to—put many children and adolescents at risk, especially in states that have banned potentially life-saving and certainly life-enhancing medical care.

CONSEQUENCES OF REACTIVE LEGISLATION

The Trevor Project, the largest suicide prevention and crisis intervention organization for LGBTQ+ young people in the United States, provides free services, including educational materials and crisis intervention, for thousands of adolescents each month. The organization also systematically tracks data and contributes to innovative research about LGBTQ+ youth. According to its research, 86 percent of transgender and gender-diverse youth reported that their mental health had suffered as a result of the legislation in the US.[23] Crisis calls rose significantly in states passing anti-transgender legislation, with more callers reporting that the legislation contributed to stress, self-harm, and suicidal feelings.[24]

Not only are transgender and gender-diverse youth distressed by the anti-trans legislation, but there has also been a simultaneous increase in violence toward transgender and gender-diverse people. The number of recorded hate crimes against transgender and gender-diverse people rose by 32.8 percent from 2021 to 2022.[25] Over three hundred transgender people were killed from 2013 to 2022 in the United States, and the two states at the forefront of anti-transgender legislation—Texas and Florida—were home to 20 percent of these deaths.[26] Even in states considered to be safer for transgender and gender-diverse people, there was a tremendous amount of violence toward the community. For example, California tracks violence in the general population, and then for the first time in 2023, tracked the percentage of transgender and nonbinary people who experienced physical violence separately from cisgender people. The state found that 27 percent of transgender people and 14 percent of nonbinary people experienced physical violence over the past year. This is significantly higher than the 5 percent of the general population that encountered violence; a 3 percent decrease from 2022. While 9 percent (a decrease from 11 percent in 2022) of the general population reported being a victim of sexual harassment or assault in the past year, sexual harassment and assault reported by nonbinary and transgender adults was flagrantly higher, at 56 percent and 40 percent, respectively.[27] This anti-trans anxiety and legislation is associated with significant violence toward the transgender community, and where data are available, shows *increased* violence.

Why is so much effort put in to shutting down safe spaces for children of all genders? Let's think about it. The 550 bills in just one year to restrict and prohibit gender-affirming care for gender-diverse children in the US, as well as bills aimed to limit the visibility of the LGBTQ+ community support, seem out of proportion given that they represent less than 2 percent of youth population. We believe that this demonstrates that the issue is not really that kids are in danger from gender-affirming care and providers. The issue is that people feel like there is something dangerous about transgender and gender-diverse people. For example, transgender girls are portrayed to be threatening cisgender girls in the bathrooms even though there have been no reported cases of this happening. To that point, here is a quote from a sign held by a transgender activist at a demonstration: "Transgender people are not dangerous. Transgender people are in danger." Yet, in terms of gender-affirming care, state and local governments in our country, as well as in other countries across the globe, have ignored the research and information coming from both the experts and the families directly utilizing this care. This reaction is clearly stemming from fear of the unknown and emerges solely from emotion rather than careful thought and investigation.

Social Gender Dysphoria

While many transgender and gender-diverse youth are suffering from gender dysphoria, gender noise, and/or gender stress, what we have seen is that any gender pathology or disorder is located within the culture rather than within individuals. This phenomenon, which we have seen in our practices, can be captured by the term "social gender dysphoria"—that it is not one's gender identity or one's body that are necessarily the basis of suffering; instead, it is the reaction from others that creates the most distress in transgender and gender-diverse children and youth. Social gender dysphoria is defined as stress or distress caused when an individual's experience of their gender is incongruous with the binary culture around them. Killian, an eighteen-year-old trans mans, offers a poignant example of social gender dysphoria and its consequences in action: "For so many kids who are trying to figure themselves out, to be told by everyone that they can't be who they are, over time, it beats them down. You shouldn't have to want to kill yourself because you just want to be who you are. People are trying to take that away from you, and it's not OK. It's not."[28]

So, what is society taking away from transgender and gender-diverse children and youth? When a society refuses to accept differences in gender identities and expressions, society takes away a person's ability to be themselves. This is done through the constant reflection of a self that is not who the individual experiences themselves to be. It is the outright denial that their identity is valid and the relentless messages telling them that they are not real, such as when others refuse to use their pronouns or name or give them access to a bathroom that feels comfortable. It is the pressure to make their gender expression and bodies match whatever society deems necessary to recognize them as the gender they know themselves to be, and this works only if their gender is girl/woman or boy/man. It is also the belittling of their self-knowledge and self-exploration.

Social gender dysphoria also includes experiences such as the profound discrimination against gender expansive people in our culture, seen in how news media platforms talk about gender diverse youth and their medical care with little attempt to make space for the voices of children and youth themselves. Discrimination also manifests in legislation aimed at limiting their rights for medical care or even legislation that has the effect of invalidating their identity. In fact, the research has found that "the strongest predictor associated with the risk of suicide was gender-based discrimination," including difficulties accessing health and medical care due to their gender identity and/or expression.[29]

What we have learned in this chapter is that the shift away from gender as a bedrock to that of fluidity and movement leaves many people stressed, distressed, confused, and challenged about their ingrown gender sensibilities. When these feelings are not reflected on and processed, they come out in reactionary responses and social discrimination, both of which are causing and worsening the social gender dysphoria seen in transgender and gender-diverse children and youth. Therefore, social gender dysphoria needs to be treated on a larger sociocultural scale so that children and youth can have a safe and spacious environment in which to explore and find themselves. As Leif, a gender fluid twenty-two-year-old, told us, "I just think that I would be a very, very different person if I hadn't had so much freedom to explore. I think that I would be a lot more sad. I think I would be a lot more confused, and I think that I would be searching for a lot more guidance. And I think the ways that I would be searching for guidance and the modes of coping would be much more extreme."

Few of us are exempt from social gender dysphoria at one time or another in our lives. To ensure that more people have the freedom that Leif has had to be gender expansive and creative, we can all unite to bring our anxieties to light and work together in the community to address our angst, support the children, and heal our social gender dysphoria. It's a win-win endeavor.

CHAPTER 4

What About This Gender-Affirmative Model?

I wish for my child, for all our children, a world where they can be who they are and become their most loved, blessed, appreciated selves.
    —Laurie Frankel, author of *This Is How It Always Is*

ALL OF THE PEOPLE WHO CAME TOGETHER to co-construct the gender-affirmative model of care wanted only to carve a path for all children to be their best gender selves. It was not just to develop a new theory to understand gender in youth; it was about putting it into practice. All of us who were involved set out to do our best to reach that goal—for each child to receive the services and support to be their most loved and appreciated gender self in a rainbow world of possibilities. You may have heard or read about the controversies swirling around this new phenomenon: "the gender-affirmative model of care." It can be very confusing. Where did this model come from? Who is it really for? In the spirit of lowering anxiety and clarifying "What is it all about anyway?" we're going to take a deep dive and share what we know and what we are continuing to learn about the gender-affirmative model.

Much of the work put into building the model has gotten tangled up in knots of confusion and misinformation among those who do not understand what the model is all about. Zooming in on the intricacies of the gender-affirmative model, let's see if we can untangle the knots to reveal a beautiful woven tapestry rather than the wrinkled mess that the lack of understanding or support for the overarching goal has encouraged it to become.

In the Beginning

In the first decade of the twenty-first century, a group from around the globe—mental health and medical providers who had been seeing growing numbers of LGBTQ+ young people in our individual offices or practices—came together to develop a standard of care. We did not anticipate the explosion in the number of youth exploring gender that was to unfold over the next decade. We also did not anticipate the shifting terrain for all children as they created their own guidebook of gender with myriad ways of knowing and being, the phenomenon that Diane had dubbed "gender creativity." Yet we were certainly aware that something was afoot. We felt a rapidly moving current both in our own country and internationally regarding "what is gender?" That current was bringing an articulate group of children and parents to our offices who were letting us know that the children had definitively embarked on their own unique gender journeys for all to see.

Many of us who have been working in this area for decades had cut our teeth in the cultural shifts of the twentieth century as gender norms, gender roles, and gender rules changed in response to the feminist movement. And still, we found ourselves opening our eyes to a new phenomenon, that was clearly in full sight. No longer was it just about William having a doll or Rosie being a riveter. It was also about who children *are*—a boy, a girl, or some other gender we had not ourselves conceived of. It was about a child with a gender that does not necessarily match what adults decided for these children when they were first born or a child who didn't stay firmly inside one binary gender box.

We witnessed this so poignantly, for example, in families where little Johnny might announce to his parents that Johnny was not a boy but a girl and wanted a Barbie doll. A progressive parent, themself raised on Marlo Thomas's *Free to Be... You and Me*, might compassionately respond, "Honey, you don't have to be a girl to have a Barbie. Boys can play with Barbies, too, and we can go buy you one." Much to that parent's surprise, Johnny would not be appeased. Quite the contrary, Johnny hurtles into a full-throttle tantrum: "YOU'RE NOT LISTENING! I *KNOW* BOYS CAN PLAY WITH BARBIES. YOU

ALWAYS TOLD ME THAT. I SAID I'M A *GIRL* WHO WANTS
A BARBIE!" Therein marks the beginning of Johnny's expansive gender journey, down a path bathed in sunshine but not without thorns
along the way. After speaking with many parents who shared this same
experience over many years, we saw a need to develop a new way of approaching every child, placing them as the nucleus of the conversation
and the leaders of the march toward the gender that they will come to
know themselves to be—either in identity, expression, or both.

We birthed what has come to be known as "the gender-affirmative
model," an approach of supporting individuals to live authentically in
their gender without privileging any outcome over another. Our model recognizes that each individual is like an artist painting their own
unique gender canvas. Those of us who took on this project came from
different disciplines, backgrounds, countries, and cultures, and from
different sexual and gender identities. Some of us were mental health
professionals, others medical providers, educators, attorneys, social
service providers, and members of the LGBTQ+ community.

Starting in the first decade of the 2000s, families and professionals
from all over the US and beyond came together for the annual Gender
Spectrum conference held in the San Francisco Bay Area. It created the
perfect opportunity for several of the participants, including me (Diane),
to begin hammering out the foundations of a new gender-affirmative
model of care and support for transgender and gender-diverse children
and their families. Similar efforts were happening among other groups
of professionals and community members elsewhere.

There were too many people involved to name them all, and we all
considered ourselves part of a pulsating, living collective organism. Yet,
to get a sense of who some of us are and how we have come together
over the years, here's a little history. In 2013, a newly formed interdisciplinary research team received a grant from the US National Institutes of Health (NIH) to study the medical and psychological effects
of puberty blockers and gender-affirming hormones. We put together
what we knew to date about the model and published the article, "The
Gender Affirmative Model: What We Know and What We Aim to

Learn."[1] All of the authors, including Diane, were members of one of the first four pediatric gender clinics in the country—Boston Children's Hospital (the country's first), Lurie Children's Hospital, University of California San Francisco Benioff Children's Hospital, and Children's Hospital Los Angeles.[2] Fast forward five years and, in 2018, I (Diane) with my coeditor Colt Keo-Meier (now Colt St. Amand) released the edited volume, *The Gender Affirmative Model: An Interdisciplinary Approach to Supporting Transgender and Gender Expansive Children*, published by the American Psychological Association. Taking a look at the list of contributors for that volume gives you a sense of the wide net of professionals who have joined together over the years to develop and enhance the gender-affirmative model, learning as we go.[3]

Together, our first task was to unlearn what we had been taught in the past about biology, children's gender development, and the role of adults in children's gender socialization. Our new schooling was to brainstorm what we were learning from scratch, what the scientific research is telling us, and what we need to discover going forward to support all children, with a particular focus on gender-diverse children and adolescents. We were responding to models for gender care that had come before us, building on those that looked promising, rejecting those that appeared to cause more harm than good—like ones that steered children away from anything that was not deemed normal in other people's eyes while ignoring the children's own voices.

Our Scout's Handbook

While sitting in meetings together, studying, brainstorming, consulting on our clinical work, joining or setting up pediatric gender programs, corresponding, coauthoring articles, embarking on research projects, and just hanging out and having fun, we came up with our basic handbook. Looking back on it, in its beginnings it was quite simple and straightforward. We generated the following basic tenets, a set of twelve that have served as the backbone of the gender-affirmative model.

- Gender diversity represents a healthy variation of human life, not a disease.

- One's gender identity may not match the sex designated to them when they were born.

- We all have a sex designated at birth, a gender identity, and gender expressions, and each person will have a unique way of putting them all together.

- Gender can be stable from early childhood and/or can evolve over the course of a lifetime.

- Gender is always an interweaving of nature, nurture, and culture; biology, socialization, and environment.

- Gender does not come in just two boxes, but in a multitude of variations.

- Gender varies from culture to culture, requiring cross-cultural sensitivity.

- For a gender creative or gender-diverse child, if accompanying psychological issues occur, like anxiety or depression, they are most likely the result of negative social responses to how that child is expressing their gender.

- Therefore, treatment, if any is warranted, should often be addressed to help and heal the surrounding environment.

- Children do better when they are accepted and supported in their gender identities and expressions; they do worse when they are not.

- Families are strengthened by accepting and supporting their children's gender.

- Living in one's authentic gender, free from aspersion and surrounded by acceptance, is a universal human right.

All of these tenets point in one direction: We are committed to promoting gender health, as indicated in the last of our twelve tenets, that everyone should have the opportunity to live authentically in their gender surrounded by acceptance and sheltered from criticism. And when a child's gender is coming into focus and it comes to ensuring their gender health, it is not for the adults to tell, but for the children to say. Once a child starts to express their gender, it is time for the adults to listen and learn how to translate, over time, what the child is saying, with the goal of creating a pathway that gives the child the best chance of being their own unique gender self.

For many years before we established the gender-affirmative model—and sometimes still in the present—gender care for children pointed in the opposite direction. Gender was prescribed and proscribed for children based on existing societal expectations and norms and on what adults were telling them about who they should be and how they should act. If a child showed tendencies to stray from the gender box society had placed them in, based on the sex designated to them at birth, there was cause for concern and a strong need to step in to "fix" the problem, teaching boys to be boys and girls to be girls and never the twain shall meet. Clinical diagnoses were created, as were therapeutic programs to provide the solution—now known as reparative or conversion therapy. This form of treatment is banned in many parts of the United States and all of Canada, but is still prevalent around the world and within religious institutions that feel bound by their beliefs and that suggest gender nonconformity is either a sin or sickness. A soft version of this model was the "Live in your own skin" approach introduced by Dr. Kenneth Zucker in Canada, which was predicated on the belief that young children, if caught early enough, still had flexible brains and could be helped to accept the gender that matched the sex designated to them when they were born, an outcome that was considered preferable to ending up transgender.

In response to Dr. Zucker's model, an interdisciplinary group of professionals in the Netherlands enlightened us to an alternative approach, articulating many pathways to gender health in which some boys may discover themselves to be girls, some girls to be boys, with positive outcomes if children are helped to be who they are.[4] The Dutch group first introduced the use of puberty blockers as a way to put a pause on a youth's puberty as they move toward consolidating their gender identity. They are indeed the originators of the gender-affirmative model. We learned so much from them, yet one way we differ is that they, when first establishing their model, promoted a wait-and-see approach until a child reaches adolescence, because many children seemed to change gender course by adolescence. Our own observations were telling us that no, some children are quite clear from an early age about their gender selves. Instead, we took a "stages" rather than an "ages" approach—a child can know their gender at any time, even in early childhood. We landed on the premise that gender does not just come in two boxes and may be infinite in all its permutations and combinations of both gender identity (who we are) and gender expressions (how we "do" our gender) and show up at any age—from early childhood through adulthood.

In 2018, when I (Diane) and Colt Keo-Meier coedited *The Gender Affirmative Model*, we tried to coalesce what we had learned to date by inviting a community of professionals who had been working to put the gender-affirmative model into practice to describe their work. In the introduction to the volume we wrote, "The gender affirmative approach has emerged and has become an ascending international model for supporting children's gender health, an effort we are proud to be a part of." We indeed all still are, although we could not have anticipated the bumps on the road ahead, which we will get to shortly. But we first want to go back in time to demonstrate that the gender-affirmative model really isn't all that new.

Barbie and the Gender-Affirmative Model

The gender-affirmative model didn't just appear from thin air. I (Diane) was one of those mothers in the 1970s who refused to buy my children the perpetually tiptoeing Barbie dolls with their retrograde messages about females and beauty. Lo and behold, I came to real-ize that embedded in Barbie, condemned by so many critics as em-blematic of patriarchy and even misogyny, was early evidence of the gender-affirmative model in action. How could that be?

No, Barbie did not represent gender in all its colors. Barbie may now come in body shapes beyond the original hourglass figure, but to date there are no trans or nonbinary Barbie dolls. Yes, original Barbie was as binary, boxed into female stereotypes as any toy could be. But she was also the hidden treasure for many young boys. I recall a young Black boy who came to see me not because gender was on his mind, but because he had been removed from his mother's care as result of neglect. He had been temporarily living with his grandmother while, with the aid of my recommendations, the courts were deciding his permanent guardianship—mother or grandmother. Yet as soon as we were alone in my office, he shyly pulled an object from his pants pock-et—a miniature Barbie, hair carefully brushed and perfectly dressed. There was no need to hide it from Grandma, who said "Whatever that boy wants and whoever he is, I'll love him forever." But moth-er was a different story: "No little boy of mine is going to be a little sissy." All this little boy wanted was to be able to express his gender, free from criticism and enveloped in acceptance, the central rubric of the gender-affirmative model. Not for this reason alone, but certainly contributing to the judge's decision, guardianship was awarded to the gender-affirming grandmother. Without his pocketed Barbie, I may never have gotten the chance to walk alongside this child in his gender journey and learn what he was trying to tell me. His was the journey of a little boy who knew he was a boy, loved being a boy, but a boy who loved Barbies, an aspect of his gender self embraced by his grand-mother but rejected by his mother.

That was the 1990s, but the story of "Barbie boys" goes way back in time. Introduced in 1959, Barbie has gone through many iterations since then. She became a mainstay in many homes as a favorite doll for little girls, and banned in many others for giving girls the wrong ideas about who women are or could be. And all the while, little boys, often in hidden pockets or behind closed doors, were alerting us to another phenomenon. Barbies were not only traditional female icons; they offered new, non-traditional opportunities for boys to express their gender. Not only can boys play with dolls, but through Barbie, they can also fantasize a life of glamor, glitter, high heel shoes, and beautifully coifed hair. Boys playing with Barbie is not to have her as a love object, but to be her, or maybe just sometimes look or dress like her. Barbie gave boys the opportunity to imagine themselves as able to express their gender as glamorously as Barbie did.

In the summer of 2023, the movie *Barbie* was released and became an instant box office hit. Shortly after its release, the *San Francisco Chronicle* published an article, "Barbie wasn't just a girls' toy."[5] In the article, we learned about many grown men, spanning ages, careers, and locations, who played with Barbies as children, dubbed the "Barbie boys." They fully understood the social norms that looked askance at boys playing with dolls, particularly Barbie dolls—it was just too girly. And yet they persevered, collecting them, sewing clothes for them, touching up their makeup, styling their hair, and building homes for them.

One Barbie boy's father put up with it until his son turned twelve in the 1970s, and then he put his foot down. As a compromise, the boy collected them instead, which he continued to do into adulthood. Another boy went underground with his Barbie play, experiencing guilt if anyone discovered his love of Barbie. Fortunately, he had a mother who fully understood one of the basic tenets of the gender-affirmative model, before those tenets were ever conceived: Children do better when they are accepted and supported in their gender identities and expressions; they do worse when they are not. This mother was aware that her son was being teased for playing with dolls. One day, she left a Barbie for him on his bed without any preconditions to play with it only in private. This green light for Barbie play is the epitome of promoting gender health within the gender-affirmative model.

Another man recalled not being so lucky. Inheriting a Barbie and her clothes from a neighbor, he was also told he shouldn't want to play with it because he was a boy. Sadly, that same year he was taken to a therapist because of his "questionable" gender expressions. He was not given the support to express gender the way that felt right to him, which is exactly what the gender-affirmative model is trying to protect against. This man, and many others in the *San Francisco Chronicle* account, channeled their early Barbie play into future careers in fashion design, theater, dance, or architecture.

So, what do cisgender boys and Barbies tell us about the gender-affirmative model?

- Gender diversity represents a healthy variation of human life. Check.

- We all have a sex designated at birth, a gender identity, and gender expressions, and each person will have a unique way of putting them all together. Check.

- Gender, whether it be identity or expressions (the latter in the case of Barbie boys), does not come in just two boxes, but in a multitude of variations. Check.

- If worried parents take their gender creative or gender-diverse child to a therapist, the child's worrisome behaviors, if present at all, can likely be the result of negative social responses to how that child is expressing their gender. Check.

- Children do better when they are accepted and supported in their gender identities and expressions; they do worse when they are not. Check.

- Living in one's authentic gender, free from aspersion and surrounded by acceptance, is a universal human right. Check.

Barbie boys, who began showing up soon after Barbie outstripped Ginny as *the* favored childhood doll, demonstrated early on that the gender-affirmative model is about all children, no matter where they live and when they were born. Who knew that Barbie would come to remind us that the aspiration is for every child to be given the opportunity to live and explore gender in the way that best suits them, not the people around them, free from harm and full of creativity.

Who Are the Providers in Your Neighborhood?

As we worked toward co-constructing the gender-affirmative model, we also began to build community-based programs, interdisciplinary medical centers, and pediatric gender clinics that would serve a child and, whenever possible, their family. We thought it imperative that each clinic see the child from every angle by offering services in many areas of knowledge and expertise. Gender-affirmative care might start with a pediatrician talking to the parents of a toddler or preschooler who has been showing some signs of gender creativity, or sometimes gender rigidity—being overly anxious about following the prescribed gender rules and regulations they perceive around them. That might be all the care a family needs to understand their child and be on their way. Sometimes it might be a teacher or school counselor who steps in, noticing that one of their students seems to be exhibiting some "gender stress" in the classroom or on the playground. At some point in a child's growing years, their parents might seek out the services of a gender clinic, where they can meet with a pediatric endocrinologist, a social worker, psychologist, or other mental health professional to talk about their child's journey and whether they need to set up some kind of a gender health plan. These professionals make up an interdisciplinary gender-affirmative team. We'd like to stress "interdisciplinary" rather than "multidisciplinary"—multidisciplinary typically refers to passing a child from a professional of one discipline to the next, while interdisciplinary means that we're all working together at the same time, creating a tapestry of our combined knowledge and expertise.

The mental health professional might offer psychological support and help if a child is exploring gender or considering a social transition to another gender, which may include changing their name, gender pronouns, attire, and so on. This involves absolutely no medical interventions and by necessity must follow the child's lead rather than be imposed by a parent or professional. Instead, both the mental health professional and the parents act as the facilitators of the social transition.

Let us illustrate with an example. Lucia was nine years old when she first went to meet with a psychologist at the local gender clinic. Before she even sat down for her first visit, she announced to the psychologist: "I know who I am, but I don't know how to do it." Creating a safe space to explore this statement over time, Lucia was able to communicate to both her parents and the psychologist that she knew herself to be a boy. Over time, she asked to get a haircut, buy new clothes, and then finally to change both name and gender pronouns—to Luke, he/him. With the support of Luke's parents, and the guidance of the psychologist, Luke chose to go to each of the classrooms at his school, accompanied by his mother, to let everyone know about his social transition.

That takes us right to the role of the educational specialist, who might be part of the gender-affirmative team. The educational expert can step in to determine what a child may need for a school to be a safe place and to also support the school faculty and staff in being gender inclusive and supportive for all the children at the school.

Let's return to Luke. The local clinic Luke was attending also had a director of education. Once apprised of Luke's plan to go from class to class asking for everyone's support in his social transition, the educational director asked Luke and his family if they would like him to talk to the teachers first about supporting Luke in his plan. Both Luke and his parents eagerly agreed, and the teachers in turn, along with the administrators, were delighted to have the director's support in helping this be a positive experience both for Luke and Luke's schoolmates.

In some instances, an attorney may be part of a gender-affirmative team, to address any legal issues relevant to a child's care. This can occur when there is disagreement between divorced parents about addressing their child's gender, when a child's school is in violation of their local gender statutes, or when a family would like guidance in requesting a legal name and/or gender marker change on their child's legal documents (specifically, passport and birth certificate). In Luke's case, his clinic had a legal director on board, and when a few years later, Luke asked to have his name legally changed and to have his legal documents say "male," the attorney was able to guide Luke and his family in this process with the courts.

If a family considers any form of medical gender care for their child once they enter puberty, a pediatric endocrinologist may have an important part to play. Most specifically, this could include puberty blockers to put a temporary pause on puberty, gender-affirming hormones to substitute the hormones that would automatically flow based on a child's designated sex at birth with those that would match the child's affirmed gender (estrogen for "feminizing," testosterone for "masculinizing"). At that point, the mental health professional steps in as well, as considerations for these forms of care are not just medical, but also psychological. The endocrinologist or physician will partner with the mental health professional who will get to know the child and learn, in partnership with the child and their family, what might be best for them going forward.

Occasionally, a gender diverse youth might express interest in learning more about surgeries, most commonly chest surgeries for youth who want a more masculine chest. Typically, however, surgeries are not the domain of pediatric care but occur after a person legally becomes an adult, which depends on where they live.

The Controversy Around the Gender-Affirmative Model

When we first set up the model, we naively thought we were pioneers. More naively, we never anticipated that less than a decade later, our straightforward model would create a tsunami of shock and outrage. There are those who perceive gender-affirmative folks not as the purveyors of good humanity bringing joy to all, but as manipulators of children's minds, looking to deform their bodies. Myths abound that we perform surgeries or hand out hormones to children as young as age five, while purposely sterilizing or even castrating young ones. Of course, this is false.

Sometime after the governor of California declared the state a "gender sanctuary state" for people of all genders in 2022, I (Diane) opened the local newspaper to read that the California Republican

Party had held a high-security meeting just to talk about gender-affirmative folks. From the reports of the meeting, we learned that we had allegedly been trained to manipulate parents and were engaged in "transgender destruction." We learned that we were sterilizing children, most of whom have mental illness, thus engaging in a form of eugenics. We learned that the end goals for gender-affirmative professionals were dark—"trans humanism, pedophilia . . . destroying the family, our culture and our society. Marxism."[6] We introduced the concept of full-spectrum thinking as a guiding principle in exploring and explaining gender. No doubt these Republicans' comments, whether mis- or disinformation, reveal these politicians have a lack of capacity to engage in nuanced thinking and instead reveal their penchant for reactive, emotional diatribes. Of course, the quoted statements are insulting to any of us involved in gender-affirmative care. But more importantly, such verbal attacks, born of fear and manipulated for political gain, are frighteningly harmful to the children who are receiving our care, which is our major concern.

Thinking back to the childhood saying, "Sticks and stones will break my bones, but words can never hurt me," we are so heartened to hear opposing messages from families receiving gender-affirmative care. First, here is a note from a family whose child had been exploring their gender over many years, with periodic meetings for consultation and guidance along the way.

> Thank you so much for all the support you've provided S and our family over the years. It was such a pleasure to meet you in person—finally! Your decades-long work and legacy have been so meaningful to so many of us, especially in this particular political moment. We're deeply grateful to have you in our lives and especially through S's transition.
>
> With deepest gratitude, B & T

The second note from a parent was sent to one of us as well as to the entire gender-affirmative team at the clinic where we work.

Thank you very much for meeting with our family today and taking the time to learn more about Z. I was really impressed by the entire care team and in particular noticed that Z felt at ease speaking to you around a topic that is so personal to him. I think this says a lot about you and the skill and empathy you bring to your work as a seasoned practitioner who recognizes the importance of this work and the discoveries it holds for young people. I also really appreciated the joy brought to the room—a joy that can be found when young people discover who they are. For all of that, I am so grateful!

In our initial enthusiasm about the gender-affirmative model, we never imagined that reflected back on us would be double exposure images of angel-devil, devil-angel. When we're engaged in gender-affirmative practices, in our work, in our families, in our close-knit communities, we can feel like angels. But to some in the world beyond those spheres, we become the devil incarnate.

Our training in mental health has taught us that strong contradictory messages about a person—on one side superlative, on the other condemning—if repeated over and over in the same time period, can make the person receiving the messages start to feel crazy. So far, we're estimating that we have been able to retain our sanity; perhaps you'll let us know as our readers! But we can also empathize with how confusing these gender shifts must be for the people who are barraged with these contradictory messages about the gender-affirmative model and the people who practice it, like the two of us. We have also learned that attacks thrown at us are often not driven by hate, but by anxiety and confusion. It can feel emotionally destabilizing when the ground is no longer firm beneath your feet as what you thought you knew about gender is challenged. Perhaps this is inevitable or unavoidable when the paradigms of gender, so deeply rooted in our culture, seem suddenly transformed into something new.

With that in mind, we'd like to explain that gender-affirmative practitioners are neither wizards nor rubber stampers luring children into a world of gender chaos, as some perceive us to be. Instead, we invite you to see us as explorers or seekers doing our part to bring into focus any particular child's gender where it might have become blurry.

Neither Wizards Nor Rubber Stampers

Over the last decade, the model has taken its place as a prevalent form of pediatric gender care. And as it has, it has been celebrated and condemned. It's as if there are two alternative realities: One where the gender-affirmative model makes everything better and another where that same model sets out to destroy the core of what you know.

In one version of the world, boys will be boys and girls will be girls—no backsies allowed. Changing your gender can't happen, or if it does, you can't speak of it or allow it to appear in the books you read. Some believe you should never say "gay" and never have drag queen library reading hours. In another version of the world, you can be yourself and embrace the gender rainbow. Either live freely and comfortably with acceptance and no aspersion, or learn to conform to what is expected. Which is right? Each of us will have to make our own weighed decisions—angel or devil or something in-between. We can tell you only what we have learned, what we have come to know. What we are about to share applies not just to providers of care, but to parents, to teachers, to anyone who has adopted the model of gender care that defines gender health as the opportunity to live in one's most authentic gender surrounded by acceptance and protected from harm.

Both as practitioners and parents, we have often been characterized as "rubber stampers," erroneously meaning that we automatically offer or agree to puberty blockers, hormones, and/or surgery to any child who asks for one of those medical interventions. Since we abide by the principle that "It's not for us to tell, but for the child to say," many believe it takes just one sentence from a child, end of discussion, and we will endorse, facilitate, prescribe whatever is packed into that sentence. Apparently, if they're a teen and they want testosterone, "like, yesterday," so be it, we pull out the prescription pad or write a letter to the doctor recommending it. If they're six and disclose they might not be the boy everyone thinks they are and please call me Sally not Sam, the recommendation must be to tell the school immediately and get right to the court to legally change their name and gender marker. The image created is of us practitioners with a rubber "APPROVE" stamp in hand to validate an order for whatever the child asks for as soon as they ask.

If this view of rubber stamping weren't egregious enough, it actually gets more nefarious than that. Some people believe the hand that guides the stamp is that of a wizard or sorcerer—one who has both the intent and the power to turn cisgender children into transgender children, with a "trans agenda"—and lure children into a cult of transgenderism. Some of you may have heard this referred to as "grooming" innocent young people toward queerness. Rumor has it that we will purposefully "castrate" children by robbing them of their fertility—putting an end to ever producing sperm or eggs by chemical means—with puberty blockers to stop the flow of adult hormones. Some even have the wild idea that we perform surgeries on young children that mutilate their genitals. After all, if we advocate listening to the children, and the child says, "Mommy, why did you give me a penis instead of a vagina?" we readily take care of that with a scalpel and some anesthesia.

The truth of the matter is that gender-affirmative caregivers are, much less glamorously, seekers and explorers. We listen, rather than tell a child what their gender is. It may take a few days, it may take many years, but the goal is always the same: To fully understand a child's gender and then provide them with the nutrients they need to live authentically in that gender.

How Do We Understand What the Children Are Telling Us?

What a child says about their gender is rarely a one-shot deal. We've discovered that gender is sometimes one of the hardest things to put into words. So, like with the early grade school ritual of Show and Tell, the experience is often one of showing rather than telling. For some children, even by the age of two or three they have already learned to read the tea leaves—gender is not something people like to hear you talk about if it goes against the grain of what they think. Such messages can easily transform into a gag rule. As psychologists, we are trained to wait until a child brings something up that they want to talk about, rather than imposing the subject on them. Through this lens, we've observed that you can wait until hell freezes over before a child operating under gender gag rules will open up about their gender, either to us, to their parents, or even to themselves. It takes patience, building trust, and breaking the cardinal rule by offering an invitation—gender is something we can talk about here. So, this can be a slow process and one in which the real challenge is in the translation—what is this child telling me about their gender that I'm not getting yet? Sometimes it's like a connect-the-dots game, sometimes a treasure hunt, sometimes a leisurely stroll, sometimes an urgent sprint.

Think of us as explorers with cameras around our necks, working to understand a child's gender so we can create a gender health plan tailor-made for this particular child. Think of us not as lone explorers, but teams—the parents and professionals as the explorers, the child facing the team as director and camera subject.

We are seekers rather than sorcerers, and the gender-affirmative model is our GPS for seeing each child as a unique snowflake, no two the same. Our only agenda is to carve pathways for each child to express their gender in creative, expansive, and growth-enhancing ways. There is no single pathway, and every person should be afforded the leeway to change direction or switch pathways as they grow and have new gender experiences. We listen, we look, we delve into a child's gender history, the gender canvas they are creating of themself in the moment, the family and community surrounding them, other events or experiences in their lives that may affect how they feel about or express their gender. At the end of that comprehensive journey, we try to ensure that the child will have all the support they need—emotional, physical, social—to live authentically in their gender as best they can.

We want to learn about each child and walk alongside them to understand what they see, what they feel from the inside out, not from the outside in. We invite you to do the same. This is where the model of the gender web can be a useful tool, allowing us to consider all the threads that come together to make any one child's gender.

But What About the Drugs?

So, what's this talk about gender-affirmative folks castrating or sterilizing children, giving them hormones at age three, performing surgeries on kindergarteners, violating parental rights by writing out prescriptions for gender-affirming hormones for youth incapable of giving medical consent, and jumping forward with irreversible medical treatments with no medical evidence to support them?

Recently, I (Diane) heard a story about a politician who said something to the effect of "But don't we get to choose our facts?" Well, no—we get to choose what we want to believe in, but when it comes to facts, our responsibility is to determine what they actually are and to correct information that is proven to no longer be true. That's what evidence-based science is about. So, let us share what we know about the facts rather than the fictions concerning medical interventions related to a youth's gender. These interventions are performed routinely around the globe with the support and direction of professional organizations like the World Professional Association for Transgender Health, the Endocrine Society, or the American Academy of Pediatrics.

By spinning their own gender webs, a subgroup of children discover at a very early age that the gender they know themselves to be does not match the sex designated to them at birth. Other subgroups of children arrive at puberty not sure about it—maybe it's a match, maybe not. Puberty brings forth a new thread of the gender web—the body—since, in puberty, secondary sex characteristics emerge as result of the sex hormones that match the sex designated to us at birth. For some youth, this becomes a wake-up call to take a new look at their gender web. For children who have known for a long time that their gender doesn't align with their sex designated at birth, and for those who are taking a new look at their gender, what they have available to them at this time in history are puberty blockers—gonadotropin inhibitors.

Puberty blockers are an intervention that simply puts a pause on puberty and are administered as either injections or tiny implants in the upper arm. This allows the child to remain in an early pubertal state to both stop the advent of an unwanted puberty or to give them more time to decide what kind of puberty they want to go through—one driven by estrogen (often referred to as female hormones) or one driven by testosterone (often referred to as male hormones). A youth is eligible for puberty blockers only once they reach the first stage of puberty—known as Tanner Stage 2—and never before that. This is the stage in which physical changes in a child's body start, such as developing breast buds or enlargement of testicles. If a child begins a puberty blocker after Tanner Stage 2, puberty is stopped in its tracks. If it is decided that a child will go off the blockers, the puberty that matches their sex designated at birth, known as endogenous puberty, will simply resume where it left off. There are no permanent physical effects of puberty blockers.

In addition to having reached Tanner Stage 2 or beyond of puberty, a child is eligible for puberty blockers only if the following criteria are met.

- The desire comes from the child, not imposed by others.

- They demonstrate a long-standing stability of a gender that does not match their sex designated at birth or are beginning to question the match.

- They have the cognitive-emotional capacity to comprehend the benefits and risks of using puberty blockers.

- Their parents or guardians are in support of the intervention.

- There is evidence of benefits to mental health through receiving puberty blockers.

- There is absence of mental health or medical issues that would not make puberty blockers a viable option at this time.

- They and their parents have received the information and have had the opportunity to discuss the possibilities for fertility preservation before beginning the treatment (because if a child starts puberty blockers at Tanner Stage 2 and then, when it is time, the child goes directly to hormones different than their endogenous puberty, it can compromise the production of eggs or sperm). For this reason, youth have the option of harvesting eggs or banking sperm prior to any medical interventions or in a hiatus between one medical intervention and another.

The second medical intervention that might be available to youth is gender-affirming hormones. This would be testosterone for those born with estrogen in their body and who want the body thread of their gender web to be a physical self with a deeper voice, facial and body hair, and other secondary characteristics that accompany a puberty driven by testosterone. For those who were born with testosterone in their body and want the body thread to consist of a physical self with breasts, softer skin, and different curves, they might request estrogen as their gender-affirming hormone. Some of these youth will have already been on a puberty blocker so that no pubertal changes have yet occurred. Others will have already gone through a puberty initiated by their endogenous hormones, so they would now be going through a second puberty. The determination for whether they are eligible for hormone treatment is the same for the puberty blockers. The main difference is that the hormones, if discontinued later, will leave some permanent effects—deeper voice, enlargement of the clitoris, and facial/body hair in a teen taking testosterone, and breasts in a teen taking estrogen.

Let's consider the opposite of the word "affirming." We have "rejecting," "negating," "repudiating." In the vehement criticisms of the gender-affirmative model, we are ironically accused of just that—negating the lack of scientific evidence supporting our medical care, rejecting the wishes and rights of parents, repudiating any scientific evidence that points to the risks of any of these procedures. This, of course, gives us pause, but the other aspect of the irony is that it is the critics of the model who are themselves rejecting, negating, and repudiating the research about the benefits of this care. This includes ignoring an article coauthored in 2023 by me (Diane) as part of a NIH longitudinal study investigating the physical and mental health outcomes in youth receiving puberty blockers and hormones at four of the major pediatric gender centers.[7] The research studies have consistently demonstrated that the kids are doing all right.

So, what about the drugs? If administered with care and caution by trained professionals in interdisciplinary teams, they can be an integral part of fortifying a youth's gender health, bringing their body in alignment with the gender they know themselves to be and the gender they want to present to the world. To sort out which youth might benefit from puberty blockers or gender-affirming hormones requires intensive knowledge by their medical providers and is not a decision made lightly. Their gender-affirmative team will dive below the surface to discover what is real, stable, and consistent in what a youth is saying about their gender, and make sure that the request for a body change isn't a solution to another life problem.

Ex Post Facto Test

Often, to test if the gender-affirmative model is working, we rely on what we sometimes dub the "ex post facto test": an assessment done retrospectively, after a child's movement to a new gender status, based on their unique gender web at work. If we got it right in facilitating a child's gender transition, and the child is now living more comfortably in a gender that is in accordance to their personal gender web, we might expect an increase in happiness and well-being. If we got it wrong, things will either stay the same or get worse. Obviously there are other life factors that can influence how a child is feeling—like a change in schools or birth of a sibling or acceptance on to the advanced gymnastics program. Yet, those of us who have been working in the field for years, with the help of reports from parents of gender creative children, have witnessed an amazing phenomenon. Never have we observed such a transformation in a child's happiness and joie de vivre as when they have received a green light to express gender as they would like, or to be the gender they've been trying to tell everyone they are, and with a thumbs-up from the people around them.

The opposite is equally true—when we got it wrong and missed what the real story was, things either look the same or the child grows increasingly uncomfortable or distressed. We once worked with a mother who leapt forward when her five-year-old expressed that sometimes he felt like a girl—buying him dresses and a long wig so he could be that girl. The problem was, he wasn't that girl. He was actually one of the Barbie boys who liked to imagine a life of glamor and glitter. And indeed, things got worse for him, with temper outbursts and anxiety. After things were slowed down and he got to go at his own pace, he calmed and was able to discover himself later as a gay boy who loved theater and stage design. Moral of the story: Let a child live in their authentic gender, and they become happier. Put up roadblocks, then not so much. And this can go in any direction.

So, What Have We Learned?

The gender-affirmative model applies to anyone who has a gender, which is everyone, even the people who say they are agender. It includes the cisgender girl who wants to be a princess, the cisgender boy who loves dressing as a princess, the cisgender boy who likes football, the cisgender girl who wants to join the football team, the transgender girl and the transgender boy who just want the opportunity to live life as they know themselves to be; the youth who are painting their own unique gender canvases, and on and on.

In 2021, a group of our colleagues at the University of Minnesota published an article[8] describing the gender-affirmative model as integrating a philosophical framework based on the evolving gender-related science with the best practices. This includes addressing the impact of stigma and discrimination on health outcomes for individuals, embracing gender diversity, and acknowledging the specific considerations for children and adolescents distinct from considerations for adults. We do hope this chapter has done justice in bringing this description to life as we have learned more and more about the children we serve.

What we haven't yet mentioned is that the challenge for everyone around the child, including the child themself, is to be able to live in a state of not-knowing for a period of time. In a culture where so many of us have been brought up to believe that gender is a bedrock and determined easily at birth by our designated sex, it is so hard to get our heads around the idea that gender can be poetry in motion, and we can't always know right away. And that is exactly what the gender-affirmative model is inviting us to do. There is no rubber stamping, grooming, or transgender agenda. The reality is just the opposite—push no agenda and allow gender not to be set in stone but an ongoing process with the child at the center as the administrator or CEO of the gender journey and we as their traveling companions. With that established, we invite you to look with us through the gender-affirmative lens to answer the questions posed in each of the remaining chapters, starting with "Where have all the young girls gone?"

CHAPTER 5

Where Have All the
Young Girls Gone?

SOME OF THE MOST SENSATIONALIZED, FEAR-INDUCING STORIES and reports on gender diversity in youth suggest that adolescent girls are being coerced into the "cult of transgenderism" and "gender ideology." Entire websites and books are dedicated to alarmist reports and warnings about how significantly more youth designated female at birth present as transgender or gender diverse than youth designated male at birth. These "girls" are portrayed as being especially susceptible to peer pressure and social contagion, which has swept them up and made them *think* they are transgender, or that they *should* be transgender in order to fit in with their peers.

The dire warnings assert that if these youth are allowed access to gender-affirming medical care—which might open the doors to receiving blockers, gender-affirming hormones, or even surgeries—they will end up regretting their "disfigured bodies." Parents are further warned that if they do not intervene, their child will continue down a transgender path. This places parents in an impossible bind. Either give your child everything they demand around their "mistaken" gender identity, including hormones and surgeries, or your child will grow to hate you and cut you out of her life. One popular book carrying these dire warnings gives parents clear steps to ensure the safety of their "girls," which include the following: 1) do not allow your child access to a smartphone or take away the one they have, 2) take big steps to separate your daughter from her gender-diverse friends. This may involve taking her out of college if necessary, or a year of family travel to keep her safe and far away from gender-diverse people who are leading her astray.[1] These are extreme measures to try to control a child's gender identity because the child differs from what their parents want or believe them to be. To separate youth from their friends because of gender identity or to isolate them from the world is likely to have negative impacts on their psychological and social well-being, including the development of and/or exacerbation of mental health difficulties. These dire warnings and extreme measures exploit fears that most parents have, such as concerns about the impact of social media on their children. At best, such guidelines to "protect your daughters" are in direct contradiction to what the current research finds, which is that family acceptance and gender-affirming care decrease mental health difficulties and improve psychological well-being. At worst, these warnings are lies and manipulation designed to evoke fear.

This narrative is rooted in sexism and some of the worst gender stereotypes of girls—exactly what we want to move away from! One part of the argument is that "girls" take advantage of this new "craze" and transform themselves into the more powerful gender—male—in order to remedy their internalized misogyny. Another piece emerges when pundits and politicians suggest, with implicit bias, that "girls" are, and always have been, highly suggestible; that they cannot possibly know their own minds at such young ages. Instead, these teen girls just fall under the influence of others. The overall message is that girls need to be protected in a way that boys do not. We see a similar SOS alert sent out about transgender women using the women's bathroom or playing in women's sports—it may be a threat to girls and young women, either to their physical well-being or the ability to compete and excel on the athletic field. Yet, the same concerns are not present, or least not to the same extent, when trans boys want to play on the boys' team or use the men's bathroom.

Despite all the alarmism and inherent sexism, we know that gender creativity is not making young girls disappear or threatening the world's population of girls and women. Remember that transgender and gender-diverse youth represent no more than 2 percent of the youth population in the United States. Instead, children and youth of *both* sexes are taking advantage of the increased cultural and psychological space to explore and express themselves. With the aim of mitigating some of the anxiety and fear, we will share what the numbers are actually telling us about the sex ratio of gender-diverse youth—that is, how many were designated female at birth, how many male. More importantly, we hope to dispel myths and calm any fears stemming from the assertion that gender-affirming care causes irreversible damage in "girls." Let's dig deeper and try to make sense of this transgender craze to focus on where children do need to be protected.

How Did This Debate Start?

The social discourse about teen girls being swept up in a "transgender craze" gained significant traction after Lisa Littman, then a professor at Brown University, published a research paper in which she penned the term "Rapid Onset Gender Dysphoria" (ROGD) in 2018. Littman presented ROGD as a subset of gender dysphoria based on parents' reports of having DFAB adolescents that "suddenly" came out as transgender or gender diverse with the onset of puberty. Littman specifically sought to investigate gender dysphoria among DFAB youth as the result of social contagion and peer pressure as well as those impacted by additional factors, such as mental health issues or parent-child conflict. The recruited parents were asked via anonymous survey if their child's coming out as transgender coincided with increased social media use and/or their child's friends coming out as transgender.

Littman's study suffered from numerous flaws. First, she recruited parents from three websites that are considered to hold cautious to negative perspectives on gender-affirming medical services for young people, and that promote the belief that "social contagion" or social exposure to transgender people causes a gender-diverse identity in youth.[2] Therefore, her research subjects came from a biased and homogenous base, in which the parents likely already believed their children's gender identities were caused by social contagion. Secondly, all conclusions were drawn from what parents reported about their children's adolescent-onset gender dysphoria because the youth themselves were never interviewed. Therefore, little is known about the actual timing of their child's gender identity discovery. Transgender people often report knowing their identity for quite some time before telling anyone. Due to the flaws in her research, Littman was forced to publish a correction in March 2019, acknowledging that "rapid onset gender dysphoria (ROGD) is not a formal mental health diagnosis," and that the "report did not collect data from the adolescents and young adults (AYAs) or clinicians and therefore does not validate the phenomenon."[3]

Another research study published in March 2023 attempted to support Rapid Onset Gender Dysphoria (ROGD) as a clinical subset of gender dysphoria. The study sought to validate that gender distress in adolescence is attributed to exposure to other transgender people, whether among their peers or through social media. The first author of the study was a parent who believed her child to be suffering from ROGD; she is not a researcher connected to any institution. Similar to Littman's research, this study recruited only parents from anti-trans websites, and therefore, all information collected was from a homogenous and biased base.[4] Fortunately, the study was retracted in June 2023 because the researchers had failed to obtain consent from participants to publish their responses.

Furthermore, research does not support the idea that gender clinics are seeing a new or different kind of gender dysphoria than before. For example, one study looked at the youth themselves and sought to test the hypothesis that ROGD is a distinct clinical phenomenon. The researchers hypothesized that youth referrals for gender-affirming medical care with more-recent onset ("rapid onset") gender dysphoria would look different than those who declared their identities at younger ages. They looked for possible expected differences in the rapid onset group, such as having more mental health diagnoses, more maladaptive coping practices such as self-harm, support from online and/or transgender friends but not parents, and lower degrees of gender dysphoria (because the gender issues weren't actually real). Controlling for age and sex designated at birth, coming out more recently in adolescence was not significantly associated with psychological distress or symptoms, mental health issues, gender dysphoria, self-harm, having gender-supportive or transgender friends, or gender support from parents. In fact, more-recent onset of gender dysphoria was associated with *lower* anxiety and lower prevalence of marijuana use, the latter considered an indicator of maladaptive coping practices.[5] The research supporting Rapid Onset Gender Dysphoria has been retracted and/or corrected to clearly state that ROGD is not a medical or psychiatric diagnosis.

In conclusion, there is *no* research that corroborates the existence of ROGD or of social contagion causing a gender-diverse identity; there is research that refutes it. In fact, sixty-two professional health organizations, including the American Psychological Association (APA) and the World Professional Association for Transgender Health (WPATH), signed a letter supporting the elimination of the term Rapid Onset Gender Dysphoria (ROGD) and similar terms as valid clinical or diagnostic terms. It lacks empirical evidence, has the potential to harm young people and cause mental health burdens, and infuses the field of psychology, not to mention the media, with spurious diagnoses.[6]

Gender Disclosure

It is common for a significant time to lapse between a child discovering their gender identity and disclosing it to their parents, as we have seen in our practices. Parents are often the last to know about their child's gender identity, which is what Diane refers to as "rapid onset parental discovery." In many of the cases we see, adolescents report waiting to tell their parents for various reasons. Some of the common ones include: because they want to be sure of their identity before disclosing, they worry about stressing out their parents, and they fear being subjected to a slew of questions that they will not be able to answer. As one nineteen-year-old transgender person said in reference to not telling their father, "I doubt he would have any clue what I was talking about or why I was bringing it to him or what it meant." This teen further explained that they are generally not out to adults because "I don't feel that, as the average person (and not in a more accepting youthful age), they would really 'believe' in nonbinary genders or understand me saying that I am one."[7]

Outside of our practices, we know that transgender youth are over-represented among the unhoused population as a result of family rejection and being kicked out of their homes. Approximately 35 to 39 percent of transgender and nonbinary youth report experiencing homelessness or housing instability (whether historically or currently).[8] So, some adolescents don't come out to their parents because they are afraid of the reaction they might receive, and in some cases, it is actually dangerous for them to come forward. No wonder so many youth might choose to withhold this information from their parents in order to stay safe (and housed) and come out only to friends, teachers, counselors, or no one at all. Research demonstrates that it is most common for gender-diverse youth to come out to therapists or medical providers first, then to their friends, and only then, to parents.[9] As Charlie (a transmasc teen) told us, they knew their parents wouldn't be supportive of their gender identity: "It [gender identity] was something that I wanted to have for myself, and I knew they wouldn't be super into it, or it'd be like a really weird thing. I wouldn't get disowned, necessarily. So, I'm grateful for that. But it would put me in a place where I would need to leave in order to keep myself alive." Despite trying to keep their gender identity a secret, their parents did find out, and Charlie had to move out of their house prior to their high school graduation.

Despite the lack of evidence that youth are coming out "suddenly" or that there is anything unique about puberty-onset gender dysphoria, the media have taken up these misinformed ideas, promoted them as disinformation, which has in turn stirred up talk of the "transgender craze."

What Is a Transgender Craze?

A social craze is similar to a fad, referring to something that is incredibly popular for a relatively short period of time, such as a fashion fad. Yet, the word "craze" differs in that it generally refers to a fad or behavior that requires much more time and emotional investment. It also tends to have a negative connotation in that it is "crazy" and unable to be understood. A light-hearted example is the rock 'n' roll craze of the 1950s in which teens spent much time and money on listening and dancing to music and attending concerts. An article from 1955 reports on how impossible it would be for adults to understand the rock 'n' roll craze that teens were caught up in. The journalist states that when you ask a teen what rock 'n' roll is, "His mouth simply falls open, a glassy look comes into his eyes, and his body begins to undulate like an earthworm with the stomachache."[10] The inherent disapproval is obvious as well as the attitude that it would be a waste of time and energy to attempt to understand youths' love of rock 'n' roll. While the craze died down, rock 'n' roll has remained, offering an interesting parallel to how some adults and media sources perceive the changing gender norms. However, unlike the rock 'n' roll craze, we maintain that gender diversity and changing norms *are* understandable to parents and adults. And most importantly, that children and youth *need* adults to understand, or at least try to, so that youth can have the space to be who they are.

The significant increase in the number of all transgender and gender-diverse children and youth as well as the rapidly rising numbers of referrals to pediatric gender clinics over the past decade is undisputed. But to refer to it as a craze—even worse, as specific to girls—completely ignores the suffering and pain that transgender and gender-diverse youth experience primarily in response to their mistreatment in our society, the immense pressure they feel to conform to gender norms that do not fit them, and the pain of repeatedly being told that they are not who they know themselves to be. As Charlie shared with us, "It definitely is [crazy-making] . . . And it affects how I view myself, and that tends to come out in not very healthy ways."

In addition to trivializing pain and suffering, this language also undermines identity exploration and development, which is one of the primary developmental tasks of adolescence. So, if we make space for youth to be whatever gender they identify with, could it become contagious?

Is Gender Identity Contagious?

If gender diversity is not a craze, can it be contagious? Some claim that the discrepancy is large and significant between DFAB youth and DMAB youth, and insist that transgender youth, especially teen "girls" are particularly susceptible to peer pressure and social contagion. To back up these claims, one writer goes as far as to compare the "trans epidemic plaguing teenage girls" with the Salem witch trials of the seventeenth century and continues the comparison with "the nervous disorders of the eighteenth century and the neurasthenia [fatigue and fainting spells] epidemic of the nineteenth century." The writer continues with, "Anorexia nervosa, repressed memory, bulimia, and the cutting contagion in the twentieth [century]. One protagonist has led them all, notorious for magnifying and spreading her own psychic pain: the adolescent girl."[11] This idea that adolescent girls could be so powerful as to have led the Salem witch trials or to have created multiple mental health disorders confuses us.

As clinical psychologists, we can tell you that cutting behaviors, bulimia, and anorexia, all continue to show up in mental health settings, some of which demonstrate rising (as opposed to falling) numbers in recent years. Let's take the example of anorexia, which has a history going back hundreds of years. Anorexia was widely covered by the media for the first time in the 1980s, and there was a big push to educate the public about how deadly eating disorders can be. The media hype occurred in response to Karen Carpenter's death from anorexia, a thirty-two-year-old singer and musician (not a teen girl). While the coverage of anorexia in the media is now sparse, the number of those contending with anorexia has remained relatively stable since 1980. By some accounts, anorexia has actually increased in recent years. However, the increase in numbers is thought to be the result of more accurately identifying those suffering from it due to increased awareness and access to treatment rather than that more people are developing anorexia.[12] Therefore, the "craze" was located in the media, not in the population. The craze ended when the media grew tired of anorexia and moved on to the next hot topic. People continue to suffer with the same issues, but the issues no longer make for novel news stories or headlines.

While it is true that teen girls and women are disproportionately impacted by eating disorders, we know that a huge contributor to the discrepancy between sexes is influenced by the messages that the larger society sends girls and women about how their bodies should look. The female body is more policed than the male body. Interestingly, transgender and gender-diverse youth are also at a higher risk of developing eating disorders. We do not think this is a coincidence given that gender-diverse youth also receive strong messages about how their bodies should look even if the ideal may be impossible for them to achieve. So, no, none of these mental health diagnoses are actually contagious, although we know that most teens seek out other teens who share their common experiences, struggles, and values.

What Is Social Contagion?

The language of "contagion" is most commonly associated with disease, warning, and danger, none of which are inherent in gender diversity. As we looked more deeply into the definition of social contagion, we found that, in fact, there are various definitions across and within disciplines, and these definitions often contradict each other or refer to very different phenomena. Apparently, neither academics nor practitioners can even agree on what social contagion is, if it exists, and even less so, how it manifests. In an attempt to synthesize the variety of research and scientific discussions, one research paper explains that social contagion is generally thought to refer to an affect, attitude, or behavior that spreads from one person to the other in a way that the recipients are not aware of external influence.[13] This is likely the closest definition to how it is used in the social contagion "theory" of gender. Yet, there is no evidence to support it, and to the contrary, there is a growing body of scientific evidence that does not support social contagion causing more youth to seek gender-affirming medical care.[14]

Since it is not based in empirical evidence, let's take up the "social" and let go of the "contagion" part. Yes, a child's environment and social relationships do impact their gender identity. Of course kids want to feel accepted and tend to seek out friendships in which they share common ground. But remember that an individual's gender web is made up of various threads drawn from nature, nurture, and culture. Yet, how these threads are woven together is ultimately an internal process, and the resulting gender web is a personal possession. If it is accurate, as we posit, that children *influence* the social context as much as the social context influences them, then it becomes illogical to claim that a gender-diverse identity is purely the result of peer influence or pressure. After all, the entire Western world exerts significant pressure on individuals to not be transgender or gender diverse. Even so, let's say that an adolescent were to seek gender-affirming care exclusively as a result of peer influence. This adolescent would *not* be provided gender-affirming medical interventions: They would be unlikely to obtain the required parental consent for treatment and would not meet the criterion of a stable gender identity cohesively situated within their psyche rather than as a solution to another life problem (in this case, the desire to be accepted in a particular social crowd). So, if the rise in number of gender-diverse children and youth is not a result of social contagion, what is causing it?

What Do the Numbers Say?

The increase in numbers of children and youth coming out as transgender and gender diverse has coincided with several sociocultural changes. First, there is a greater awareness of gender diversity and gender dysphoria in Western culture. There is also a greater availability and visibility of gender-affirming care and increased insurance coverage for gender-affirming care for youth. As more youth present as gender diverse, the more the culture shifts to represent the actual population of gender-diverse people, which then opens up more space for gender exploration. So, it makes sense that more gender-diverse youth and their families are seeking care. In terms of a difference in the sex ratio of patients showing up at pediatric gender clinics, it is true that many gender clinics report that the number of DFAB youth referrals has increased, and in many cases, has surpassed the number of DMAB youth who present for care. This corresponds to what we have observed in our own practices: There has been a shift from predominantly DMAB youth fifteen years ago to a more even spread across both sexes. But while the number of DFAB youth at gender clinics is greater, when one examines the numbers across the general population of transgender and gender-diverse youth as opposed to only those showing up at gender clinics, the numbers actually show slightly more youth designated male than female. This is consistent with the overall US population.[15] DFAB youth outnumber DMAB youth in referrals to pediatric gender clinics; however, there are more DMAB transgender and gender-diverse youth than DFAB youth in the general population.

It's important to note that not all families are seeking gender-affirming medical care when they visit a pediatric gender clinic, and there are no medical interventions for prepubescent children. In terms of gender diverse adolescents, not all even want medical intervention. Additionally, there are some pediatric gender clinics in the US that don't have the ability to provide gender-affirming medical care due to local laws and legislation. Looking across the pond, the UK is presently in a state of flux as it transitions pediatric gender services from the closed Tavistock Gender Identity Development Service (GIDS) with the introduction of more regional service hubs under the auspices of the National Health Service, with differences of opinions among providers regarding what medical options should even be provided.[16] Remember pediatric gender clinics usually employ an interdisciplinary team, so many families arrive for information, mental health support, social work services, and support in accessing supplementary services, such as educational and legal support. In addition, some studies show that medical interventions have *decreased* over time despite rising numbers of patients in these clinics.[17]

Why a Discrepancy in Numbers?

There are many possibilities for this shift in referrals in which DFAB transgender youth outnumber the DMAB youth. The most likely cause is a shifting cultural terrain that opens the door with expanded opportunities for youth to explore their gender identities and contemplate ways in which they can express themselves. Even so, this terrain impacts who publicly comes forward and identifies as transgender or gender diverse. For example, in Western culture, DFAB individuals will most likely be allowed more flexibility and freedom in their gender expression than DMAB individuals. In our society, it is generally more acceptable for a girl to don masculine clothing and excel in sports, than for a boy to wear a dress or be interested in princesses, which is still highly discouraged or even disciplined.

Therefore, a girl might feel more freedom to express her gender and preferences with little experience of having the sex designated for her being a limitation to her self-identity and expression. Yet, when puberty begins, she may begin to feel more confined by how others see her and how she begins to be treated differently. Puberty for designated female children usually begins with the development of breast buds that are visible for all to see. This may make puberty more distressing for DFAB youth as opposed to DMAB youth whose puberty usually begins later and with the first change being that the testicles and scrotum (skin around the testicles) begin to get bigger and pubic hair forms on the base of the penis, which remains private and unseen.

One possibility is that more DFAB adolescents might seek gender-affirming medical care since testosterone provides masculinizing features even at lower doses or if taken only for a relatively short period of time. For example, one's voice can deepen permanently even if testosterone were to later be discontinued. In this way, testosterone provides more opportunities for a youth to acquire the goals they have for their body and its presentation than estrogen does for DMAB teens. This is especially true for those who have already gone through puberty, leading more DMAB youth to feel less optimistic about what a gender clinic could offer them since their deep voice, for example, cannot be altered. Estrogen also needs to be taken at a full dose and for some time before there are noticeable bodily changes (such as breast development).

Another possibility is that DMAB children tend to show up at gender clinics at earlier ages, often before puberty, because families may become concerned if they have a little boy who is not conforming to gender norms. DFAB children are allowed much more flexibility in how they present their gender, so it is likely less of an issue for them until they reach puberty when their gender box becomes more restricted and/or the world responds to them differently. There is also the very real threat of violence and bullying for all gender-diverse youth, but DMAB youth are at the most risk of being the target of violence. This may prevent some DMAB youth from sharing their identities with others or seeking gender-affirming medical care that might out them in unsafe situations. For these reasons, the numbers of DFAB youth who identify as transgender, nonbinary, or gender diverse may be inflated while the numbers of DMAB youth may be underreported.

Bullying and Violence

All this talk of a transgender craze suggests that there is something alluring about taking up a gender-diverse identity even if it is not felt to be a true one. Yet, it is hard to imagine that many young people would choose to go through the distress of coming out as transgender or gender diverse with the sole conscious desire being just to fit in with a group of peers. It is true that adolescents try on identities, and this is one way that they come to know themselves. Yet, a *consistent* and *persistent* gender-diverse identity suggests that it is not merely a "trying on" but instead is an authentic identity. Regardless, it is important to note that transgender and gender diverse youth are much more likely to be bullied or harassed at school than their cisgender counterparts. The US Centers for Disease Control and Prevention (CDC) reports that transgender students are more likely to describe feeling unsafe at school; on the journey going to and from school, being bullied, being threatened or injured with a weapon, being forced to have sex, and experiencing physical and sexual dating violence. Nearly 25 percent of transgender students report being threatened or injured with a weapon compared to only 6.4 percent of cis boys and 4.1 percent of cis girls.[18] Another study found that 86 percent of transgender youth reported being bullied, victimized, and/or harassed as a result of their gender.[19] which is in line with a study from the United Kingdom that found that 86.5 percent of transgender youth seeking gender-affirming care reported being bullied because of their gender identity, predominantly in schools.[20] Furthermore, transgender youth who experienced victimization due to their gender identity were three times more likely to have missed school in a given month than other students.[21] When transgender youth were not given access to either a restroom or locker room that fit with their gender identity, they were more likely to experience sexual assault compared to those who did not have these restrictions.[22]

One DFAB and gender creative teen, Rae, shared with us how much their gender identity initially made them feel really confident and positive once they were able to come out as gender diverse. Yet, at school Rae described, "The bullying was relentless, and it really took a toll on my mental health. I remember sitting in the cafeteria crying because these boys were disgusting toward me and my other trans friend. They would tell me to kill myself." Rae went on to describe the toll the bullying and discrimination took on their mental health and points out that "most of the reason was the bullying. It wasn't because of my identity."

Another teen, Charlie, who is transmasculine, described an incident on the subway in which they and their trans friend were threatened by a man with a knife, who repeatedly said, "I'm going to kill you. I'm going to get you tonight." As Charlie describes, "He kept getting closer. It was the longest three minutes of my life" waiting for the next subway stop so that they could escape. We think that if any of our teens need protection around gender identity, it is from the violence directed toward them, not from other gender-diverse youth.

What If They Regret It?

Because youths' brains are still developing and changing at a rapid pace, we worry that they will make rash decisions in any domain of their lives and may be sorry later. This worry goes through the roof when it comes to trans and gender diverse youth who make decisions for gender transitions, particularly medical ones, that are either partially or totally nonreversible. Yet, read what seventeen-year-old trans youth, Syrus, says on this very topic: "I worked really hard to be able to transition . . . I dealt with bullying at school, and people being mean to me just because I exist. If I can deal with that, I know who I am. I'm not going to go back."[23]

Syrus represents the sentiments of many, but regardless of these affirmations about their commitment to their gender transitions, endless talk has been devoted to adolescents and adults "detransitioning" or reverting to the sex designated to them at birth due to regret over gender-affirming medical transition (i.e., hormones and surgeries). But in reality, it is extremely rare for adolescents or adults to express regret over their gender-affirming medical transitions even if they later go on to identify with their sex designated at birth. Even so, "detransitioners" are often featured in media or spoken about among legislators as though they are the norm rather than the exception, and their stories are used in an attempt to discredit gender-affirming care. On the flip side, we have never seen a similar reaction to the higher incidence of cisgender individuals who have later regretted their "gender enhancing" surgeries, such as a face lift or a breast augmentation, with a cry to shut down all cosmetic surgery because it can cause regret.

Yet, research and our own professional experience support that de-transitioning, which we prefer to speak of as "re-transitioning," is rare, and even when it does happen, it is not necessarily about regret. In some cases, the shift is simply a part of the individual's evolving gender identity. Some may have wanted or needed gender-affirming medical care for only a relatively brief time in order to treat their gender dysphoria. One example may be a DFAB individual who takes a low dose of testosterone long enough to achieve some permanent changes, such as a deeper voice and peach fuzz. These physical changes are just enough to significantly reduce their gender dysphoria, so they stop hormone treatment. Other individuals might discontinue gender-affirming medical care due to financial constraints and/or a change in their ability to access ongoing medical treatment. There are also some medical conditions that can prevent the safe use of gender-affirming hormones and may require an individual to discontinue use. Still others might discontinue care because they find that medically transitioning has made their gender diverse identity more obvious in places, and they are finding it no longer safe to be out in this way. Others are simply embracing a new shape to their gender web, with no regrets about the steps that have led them there.

Of course, there are the claims that puberty-onset gender dysphoria in DFAB youth makes them more at-risk for regret, given their status as minors and lack of a long history of gender-diverse identity, but we find the opposite to be true. In fact, adolescents who present with persistent gender dysphoria after starting puberty almost always persist in their gender identity in the long-term, whether or not they were provided gender-affirming medical care.[24] It is more common for children who came out as transgender under the age of six to evolve to their gender associated with the sex designated at birth by the age of ten than it is for those who came out as adolescents.[25] Approximately 1.9 to 3.5 percent of transgender youth receiving gender-affirming medications at specialized gender clinics discontinued treatment[26] and in some cases, we don't know the specifics of why they stopped attending appointments. For all we know, they switched providers.

Most adults who stop gender-affirming hormones report doing so for reasons unrelated to a change in their gender identity. Instead, adults most commonly cite external reasons such as pressure from family, difficulty obtaining employment, or gender-based discrimination.[27] For example, one survey of 17,151 transgender adults found that 13 percent reported a history of re-transition, which did not necessarily carry any feelings of regret. The majority (82.5 percent) of those who reported a history of re-transition, cited external reasons, particularly pressure from unsupportive family members and societal stigma as opposed to a change in their gender identity.[28] A meta-analysis of twenty-seven different studies that collectively pooled 7,928 adolescent and adult transgender patients who underwent any type of gender-affirming surgery found that the prevalence of regret was only 1 percent.[29] Let's compare this to a meta-analysis of studies looking at regret after elective surgeries that are not gender-related, and we find a shocking 14.4 percent of patients expressed surgical regret.[30] That's a huge discrepancy, indicating that there is an uncommonly low regret among gender-affirming surgery patients versus other types of elective surgeries. For those who did regret gender-affirming surgery, the most common reason given was because of their feelings about the response of the world around them, such as from their family or social environment. Some patients chose to reverse their gender role to achieve social acceptance, receive better salaries, and preserve relationships with family and friends.[31]

As we can see, regret during and after gender-affirming care is rare and not a creditable reason to prevent access. It is also not disproportionately impacting teenage girls. While we pay attention to differences in the sex ratio among transgender and gender-diverse youth, the fact of the matter is that gender diversity is everywhere. With that said, let's turn to the most important voices who have been left out of much of the media coverage—the voices of transgender and gender-diverse children and youth themselves.

CHAPTER 6

Teach Your Parents Well
The Children Speak

*Me: What would you say to someone who says, "If you have
a penis, you're a boy"?*
*M. (age seven): I would say, "How do you know? It's not
a rule!"*

—Marlo Mack, *How to Be a Girl*

WHEN IT COMES TO EXPLAINING GENDER, CHILDREN are
our best teachers. For many of them, the gender rules that we grew
up with do not make sense. Certainly, these new norms of gender
didn't just emerge out of whole cloth. Multi-generations of gender
evolution are passed down to them. They in turn react with their
own gender creativity. What do they know? What can they teach us?
What are we teaching them? A child in China may teach us something completely different from a child in Nigeria, who in turn may
see things differently than a child in Australia, a child in Colombia,
a child in Kansas, a child in Los Angeles or London. Despite these
differences, are there universal truths that we can extract to explain
youths' evolving relationship with gender?

Learning from an American Child

When Alexander was eight years old, he began to wonder whether he
might be a girl rather than a boy. From as early as he could remember,
he always gravitated toward his older sister's dolls and dress-up clothes,
leaving his own trucks and junior baseball mitt lying untouched on his
toy shelf. Over time, he established that his favorite color was pink,

and no shirt was worth wearing unless it had a butterfly applique on it, especially a butterfly sparkling with glitter. One day, he was wearing one of his pink sparkly butterfly shirts to school, feeling great about himself. Then came recess. Two older boys approached Alexander on the playground, boys who he was acquainted with from his after-school program. One of the boys got in his face as his friend cheered him on and announced menacingly, "Hey, you can't wear that shirt. Boys can't wear pink. Pink is for girls." Alexander looked each of the older boys right in the eye and responded, without missing a beat: "Well, I'm a boy. And I'm wearing pink. So, I guess boys can wear pink." He then calmly walked away, leaving the two older boys perplexed and tongue-tied.

When we reflect on the bedrock as well as the shifting terrain of gender for the youngest among us, all three of these children are standing on that ground. For the two older boys, it's the bedrock: Pink is for girls, never for boys. For Alexander, it's shifting terrain: Those rules don't make sense; if a person likes pink, they should get to wear it. No separate rules for boys and girls.

This is what actually happened between Alexander and the two boys. But let's imagine for a moment if the following had occurred: Alexander didn't walk away. Being an intellectually curious child, he might have stayed on to point out to the two older boys that in the olden days, pink was actually a boy's color—up until the 1920s, clothes catalogues advertised pink for boys' attire. Back then, pink was considered a masculine color and a variation on the "mother" color of red for men. The primary color red was perceived to mean ardent, passionate, active, aggressive. But forget about all of that, too, because Alexander would then explain that he had no desire for anyone to think of him as more aggressive or ardent, but rather as a gentle boy who just likes pink—and sparkly butterflies. And to round it all off, he might have asked the two boys who were giving him grief, "Don't you know about the *Barbie* movie? *Everyone's* wearing pink to go see it. So, I guess a lot of boys are wearing pink."

By the time Alexander would have finished his lecture, the two older boys may have fled, rolling their eyes as they dashed away. Or maybe it would have been an opportunity for the boys to think over this "pink isn't for boys" thing and wonder if the gender rules they had been taught were working for them as much as they believed. Wouldn't it be nice to be freed from feeling so pumped up all the time and not compelled to serve as the gender police on the playground?

We share these "what-ifs" for Alexander and his schoolmates not just to bring you to an alternative reality, but to share that many youth who we've gotten to know actually delight in this discovery that pink used to be a boy's color/blue a girl's color. Indeed, if they are a boy who likes pink, they go on to use that information in their "gender toolbox" when dialoguing with other youth who give them grief about their color choices. And if they are a boy who thinks they're not supposed to like pink, we've watched them stop short at this newfound information and even drop their own "gender policing."

A Child Calls Out from Another Generation

Let's leave Alexander and his peers for the time being and do a little time travel. For anyone who was around in the early 1960s, you may remember when Scout came on the scene, the first-person narrator from Harper Lee's novel *To Kill a Mockingbird*, published in 1960. Whether on the written page, the stage, or the Hollywood screen, Scout, a child growing up in a fictional town in the Deep South, was etched in our collective memory as the girl who challenged every mid-century norm for how a girl was supposed to look, act, and feel.

About the play she and her older brother Jem produced, she says, "I reluctantly played assorted ladies who entered the script. I never thought it as much fun as Tarzan." About the boy she planned to one day marry, who professed his love and then neglected her, she says, "I beat him up twice but it did no good." About her Uncle Jack's question, "You want to grow up to be a lady, don't you?," Scout expresses "Not particularly." About her aunt Alexandra's fanatical insistence that Scout wear dresses so she could be the sunbeam in her father's lonely life, Scout's retort is, "One could be a ray of sunshine in pants just as well." About the reaction of that lonely father, Atticus Finch, Scout narrates, "When I asked Atticus about it [what Aunt Alexandra had said], he said there were already enough sunbeams in the family and to go on about my business, he didn't mind me much the way I was."

Who was Scout? A girl. A girl who planned to marry her male friend, Dill, when they grew up. A girl who did not abide by the gender rules or gender attire of her time. A girl pressured by those around her to be more of a lady. A girl whose father said—you're fine the way you are. A girl who felt the tension between how she wanted to "do" her gender and the messages from the outside world about how she was supposed to be acting more like a "lady." A girl all of us loved then and now. A girl created by a writer who might have been fully aware that traditional gender tropes were already beginning to tumble as the 1960s rolled in and Betty Friedan would soon publish her book, *The Feminine Mystique*, which became a staple on many people's bookshelves. Whether Harper Lee foresaw that shifting of gender or not, she certainly knew how to capture the imagination of her audience, then and now, by placing Scout, a gender creative child, as a main character in her poignant tale of the racist Deep South. Through a fictional child character that numerous readers, including the older author of this book, identified and resonated with, we find evidence that children's gender creativity and this new gender world has been in the making for many, many years.

Who Are the Genders in Your Neighborhood Today?

By now we hope you recognize that gender is highly individualized, everyone has their own unique gender web, and there are too many genders to count. Instead, we'll introduce you to just some of those who live in your neighborhood. As much as we would like to let the children speak in their own words, we are sensitive to the turmoil swirling around us in the face of the present political attacks on gender creative children, and so we're taking every precaution to preserve their confidentiality and ensure their safety if they are living among those who are not always particularly kind toward them. As we mentioned in the first chapter, we have changed all names and identifying information and in some cases have created composites of children we know as an extra precaution.

THE BOY WHO CAME INTO HIS OWN, FELL OUT, AND CAME BACK

Sam is now fourteen. He knew from early childhood—before he could even make whole sentences—that "girl" (who everyone thought he was, based on what his body looked like when he came into the world) didn't feel right. He kept it to himself until he got a little older and evolved into the transgender teen he is today. Recently, he began a course of gender-affirming hormones (testosterone) to allow him to have a puberty that matches the boy he is. This was done after careful thought and evaluation that included him, his family, and his team at a pediatric gender clinic, in compliance with the gender-affirmative model.

He has been so much happier since he began noticing the changes brought about by testosterone—a deeper voice, a bit of peach fuzz above his upper lip. But he's also a studious type who reads the news every day. He knows there are people, some of them medical experts, who say he's too young to know his gender with certainty and who evaluate him to be at risk for regret and a bad outcome if he starts taking a medication, in his case testosterone, that has permanent effects. These people assert their opinion even though they have never met Sam, or any other youth just like him, a child who discovered early in life that the gender he was did not match the sex that the adults designated to him when he was born. Up until that moment, he had consistently felt secure in his self-knowledge, "I am a boy." But now, for the first time, he is beginning to have doubts: What if I'm just a kid and I'm wrong? What if those critics are right?

It is common for young people to have doubts when they cross the threshold into adolescence, and of course, we want all doors to open for new self-discoveries as youth enter this exciting but precarious transitional stage between childhood and adulthood. Yet, that is not what is happening for Sam. The bedrock that he believed his true gender identity to be breaks under the barrage of scrutinizing skepticism and opinions that are based not on science but belief. Left in its stead is a rocky hillside where Sam is warned by outside elders that each step might catapult him into a pit of self-destruction—hormone effects he can never undo, years of his life he might have wasted living in the "wrong" (i.e., affirmed) gender. With the enervating whispers of all those gender doubters reverberating in Sam's ears, an old tune from his childhood floats in. It's Kermit the Frog soulfully and sadly singing like an old bard, "It's not that easy bein' green." Just substitute "bein' trans" and you've got the twenty-first century version of Kermit's song for Sam, until Sam remembers the words to the second verse of Kermit's song, which teaches us that it's fine to be green because that's who Kermit wants to be, and so he'll do just fine being green.

A boy is not just what Sam wants to be, but who he *knows* himself to be. Sam teaches us that he can know his gender, did know his gender, but he's also just a kid influenced by what the adults, even if misguided, keep saying about him—not even to his face, but in written and spoken word by misinformed pundits and politicians who have never even met him. Thank goodness for Kermit and *Sesame Street*, an old and dear childhood memory that brings Sam back to his point of equilibrium: I am a boy who has come into my own.

IT'S ALL JUST SO AWKWARD

Margo, a middle school student and a very sensitive and private youth, lives in a northern state in the US that is pushing to ban pediatric gender care. She has known from early childhood that "girl" did not feel right. By the age of four, she was refusing to wear skirts or dresses. Her childhood was easy in this regard, until puberty started, and she plunged into despair as she watched her body transform into one that felt gruesome to her. She was able to get puberty blockers to stop any further puberty from happening while she sorted out her feelings about her gender. And she still hasn't. Margo knows she doesn't feel like a girl, she knows she never wants estrogen in her body, she knows she's delighted that, thanks to her cropped hair and choice of clothing, people who don't know her assume she is a boy. She is troubled by not being able to make a decision about socially and medically transitioning to be the boy she knows herself to be in her heart. Margo doesn't doubt that knowledge, but she believes that it would jeopardize her relationships with all the people she cares about, even though they have all told her that they will love her no matter what. She's not worried that she doesn't know her true gender self, but that she will feel awkward asking the people around her to recognize her as a boy and will never be able to feel comfortable with them again, even if they are all okay with it. Margo's situation reminds us that a child's gender doesn't unfold in a vacuum. Where it ends up is deeply interwoven between self and other—the child and the world around them, both intimate and far removed.

BUT I LOVE BARBIE AND MY BROTHER LOVES TRUCKS

Amanda is eight years old. She and her twin brother, Frankie, live with their single mom, Gloria, who works at a non-profit organization in a small city in Canada. Gloria has always wanted her daughter to grow up strong and assertive, and never have to suffer from the repressive norms of the school she had attended from kindergarten through twelfth grade. For her, girls were taught to be "ladies," prepared to be homemakers, and were required to wear dresses to school, including to all school-related activities, even on the coldest, snowiest days. Gloria was determined to provide her daughter with all the freedoms she never had and to reject all archaic or oppressive gender norms, which included no Barbies, and that frills are for doilies, not my daughter.

As for Frankie, Gloria was determined to help him escape toxic masculinity and discover the "feminine" in him. She lined his toy shelf with cute little stuffies and books about gentle boys, like *Sparkle Boy* and *Clive and His Babies* and *Pink Is for Boys*. The books lay untouched. All Frankie wanted was a shelf full of Tonka trucks, and maybe some toy soldiers and even a little gun—just a pretend one, of course. All Gloria wanted was for Frankie to grow up to be the kind of man she always wished she could have known but never had the opportunity to meet—kind, able to express his feelings, nurturing, and favoring affection over aggression. Yet, Frankie preferred to play with the toys he was drawn to, like the toys all the other boys played with.

We all want children to have parents who love them and have dreams for them, but children, if given the chance, will let you know when those dreams overpower their own. This tension can be a real downer, even a catalyst for open warfare. In Amanda and Frankie's case, for whatever reason, they each gravitated toward what could be labeled as traditional gender norms. Amanda liked frills and anything pink, and she would have traded any toy just to have one Barbie to play with. Frankie wanted only a *vroom-vroom* life with all his *vroom-vroom* friends, and a camouflage jacket so he could look tough and cool.

Frankie and Amanda are just two of our neighbors in the global world of gender. Were they gravitating toward "traditional" gender expressions simply to individuate or challenge Gloria's expectations for them to be gender nonconformers? Maybe. Were they too influenced by the culture around them and intent on conforming to avoid rejection and solicit acceptance? Maybe. As twins, did they feel internal pressure to differentiate themselves from each other? They may have shared the same womb and the same birthday, but they may have also wanted to let the world know that "we are two very different people—I am girl, he is boy; let us show you with our actions." Well, maybe.

Yet, in getting to know Amanda and Frankie better, none of those possibilities seemed to be in play. Instead, they were a close pair who loved their mother very much but thought all her "Free to be you and me" stuff was just silly. In the children's view, it would have been better if Gloria could just let them be free to express their true gender selves—a cisgender girl who loved pink, frills, and Barbie, and a cisgender boy who loved trucks, rough play, and hated the color pink.

PLEASE LISTEN!

A group of teens from the US have spoken publicly about attempts (and successes) in dismantling gender-affirmative care and social supports for gender-diverse youth. L.W. is one of the youth who is speaking out publicly about her right to the care she needs. At the time of this writing, she is fifteen and identifies as a trans girl. L.W. has served as one of the plaintiffs in a lawsuit against the state of Tennessee in response to a legislative ban on pediatric gender care. What did this ban mean to L.W.? "I don't even want to think about having to go back to the dark place I was in before I was able to come out and access the care that my doctors have prescribed for me. . . . I want this law to be struck down so that I can continue to receive the care I need, in conversation with my parents and my doctors, and have the freedom to live my life and do the things I enjoy."[1] If the law was to be put in place, L.W. would have to stop her gender-affirming hormones within nine months of the start date of the law. For L.W., the thought of being denied life-saving care is a terrifying one.

In the same year that Tennessee successfully pushed through their ban on pediatric gender care, Nebraska was attempting to follow suit. Their bill would criminalize medical gender care for anyone under the age of nineteen. A twelve-year-old transgender boy, Ash Homan, stood up to have his say on the hearing floor, urging lawmakers not to ban transition-related care for transgender minors. He had this to say to the lawmakers: "People introducing and passing these laws underestimate how much a child knows about their own body and about their own brain."[2] It should be noted that his mother is Senator Megan Hunt of the Nebraska legislature. Here is a reporter describing Ms. Hunt giving words to her son's experience.

> Before Ash transitioned, Ms. Hunt said her child was often depressed, but in recent years he has flourished. He's popular in school, has a busy social life and recently started a club for fellow students who are aspiring authors . . . It was like the clouds parted . . . He's having a great childhood, and he wasn't before.[3]

Alx Montgomery is another transgender youth living in Nebraska, five years older than Ash. Alx began his gender transition when he was eleven. Taunted and harassed by peers and extended family, by age twelve he made a suicide attempt. He survived, and by age sixteen had legally changed his name and began a course of testosterone, preceded by extensive psychotherapy and careful reflection. He credits that experience with significantly improving his mood and outlook.

> They'll never understand how it feels to look at yourself in the mirror after being on hormones for a few months and you finally start seeing changes. . . . Suddenly you're smiling at your appearance instead of hiding away.[4]

In the UK, youth have their own battles to face. As of June 2023, less than half the population polled thought that youth should have access to gender-affirming medical care or counseling.[5] So, please listen to these youth as well. One of the main tenets of the gender-affirmative model is that every person has a right to live in the gender that is most authentic to them, free from aspersion and surrounded by acceptance. By appearing before legislative bodies in their home states, these young people boldly embrace the principle not only by knowing it but by acting on it as they educate lawmakers about the reality of gender, in all its iterations, as a phenomenon to be celebrated and supported, rather than vilified and decimated.

I'M JUST A KID

Recently, I (Diane) met with a family from a state that had banned pediatric gender care. The clinic where eleven-year-old Stephan had been receiving care in the form of puberty blockers was suddenly closed and so Stephan's family quickly researched care options in other states. This family was fortunate to have enough resources to travel to another state to be able to secure continuing care for their child. Stephan would have been devastated to learn that they would have to stop their puberty blockers after such psychological improvements since starting them the year before and being assured that they would not experience unwanted changes from an endogenous puberty. The family discovered they would be able to receive care in the state of California and set up a meeting with me. During this visit, which included meeting Stephan along with both his parents, I asked the family how they were doing emotionally after their state's laws banning gender care were put into effect. Before the parents had a chance to respond, this wise child immediately jumped in and shared, "I'm only eleven. I don't know about laws." Duly noted: Stephan is only eleven and eleven-year-olds should get an opportunity to live their life free from impediments and complete with opportunities to grow and thrive. We owe thanks to this gender creative child for reminding us that children need growth and expansion, but also protection.

How Do Children Learn About Gender?

Every child is gender creative, because every child is painting their own gender canvas, based on nature, nurture, and culture. And they're not just painters. For every child entering the world, gender is something they are, something they do, something they feel, something they tell (or don't tell), something they learn, something they teach. If you ask a child how they know their gender, you can expect that they might first look at you blankly and respond, "Well, it just is." Actually, it is, and it isn't. It's a child's own possession, as we've heard from each of the young ones' accounts described in this chapter, but it is also a relational dance between the child and the people most dear to them, starting with their parents or primary caregivers. What does this gender choreography look like? Unbeknown to the psychologists who developed Attachment Theory, they—with particular thanks to John Bowlby and Mary Ainsworth as the father and mother of the theory[6]—gave us the invaluable gift of one important construct to help us understand how a child first learns about both their own and others' gender.

THE FEEDBACK LOOP

Attachment Theory, one of the most heavily researched aspects of developmental psychology, demonstrates that there is a feedback loop between a child and their parent. Starting from birth, the infant influences the parent just as the parent influences a child. We tend to think of parent-child relations as more of a one-way street—children come into the world totally dependent on their parents, and parents will influence them in positive or negative ways. Yet for those of us who have raised more than one child, we are sometimes taken aback when we experience the extent to which our children shape us, and how different our parenting becomes for each of our children. For example, the docile baby is a vastly different influencer than the colicky baby. One means we are copasetic in the rocking chair, the other leaves us red-eyed and monstrous after a sleepless night.

Focusing on gender, parents no doubt shape their child's understanding about gender in the world and in the child's own life. At the same time, the child is sending out signals from their own mind that in turn influence how the parent responds in the earliest months of their child's life to shape their evolving gender web. Science is still working on explaining to us *why* that happens, but observational studies can verify *that* it happens.

Originally we all thought that a baby is designated a sex, boy or girl, at birth; the child then learns that they are a boy or a girl because parents call them such, and then when they get to be about three years old, they start learning what it means to be a boy or a girl. There is certainly partial truth to this, but we forgot to factor in that the child's gender is not just a piece of moldable clay to be shaped by parental and societal expectation. It may or may not match the sex designated at birth. If it is not a match, a child as young as one or two will begin to let that be known, not necessarily in words but in action. Many of us hold the poignant memory of the 2007 Barbara Walters *20/20* special on transgender children (the first ever), showing early footage of a transgender girl as a toddler unsnapping her onesie so that it could look like a dress rather than shorts.

The lesson we have all learned from the children is to listen to them, and not tell them about their gender. Recall that if we don't, we grab the threads of the gender web from their hands and leave the child feeling tangled. By listening to them, we emphasize that they know something we may not, and that is precisely where the feedback loop comes into play—the child tells, the parents listen, and then they reflect back their own responses to what the child has communicated about their gender.

Let's go back to Margo. She is still in the process of sorting out her gender and how she wants to live it going forward. But way before she started middle school, in her earliest years, both of her parents were already noticing some "gender breadcrumbs" along the path. In her toddler years, she was always shuffling around the house in her father's work boots. She loved making a milk moustache so she could be just like him. Her parents, who had two older children, insisted, "We raised her just like the other two, but this one, as soon as she had words, would announce, 'Want boy, not girl.' We swear, we didn't make this happen. We were just following her lead." Wherever that lead came from, Margo, in her earliest years of life, was already shaping her parents to raise her differently from her older siblings, as a girl who may be a boy. And they obliged by giving her the message back that whoever she was would be the person they would always love. That suited Margo well, but then in middle school, in the midst of her great angst about starting puberty, she threw a curveball by letting her parents know that even though they said those things, she was still afraid that if she changed her gender it would always be "awkward" between them. This was said by a child who, in every respect, was always seen in the outside world with a haircut, clothes, and appearance as a boy, never as a girl. And so the feedback loop goes round and round.

MIRRORING

A child gets an image reflected back to them about who they are and how they are perceived. D. W. Winnicott, a renowned pediatrician and psychoanalyst, described mirroring as the parent returning the image of the child that is there to be seen. If, instead of reflecting back a genuine image of the child, the parent imposes the image they want to see, the child may become confused, agitated, angry, or give up in defeat. If the parent reflects back an image of the child as they know themselves to be, the child feels recognized, acknowledged, embraced, and fortified in their own sense of who they are.[7] It's the same as when you look in a mirror. If it is distorted, like the mirrors in an amusement park funhouse, you may be surprised, even mortified, by the image of you that is reflected back. If the mirror is in perfect condition, you may still not like what you see, but the image is real—that *is* you. But "mirroring" as a verb, a transaction between two people, is not just about reflecting back how you look; it is a deeper phenomenon about reflecting back who you are.

Applying this to gender, children depend very much on their elders to mirror back to them what the adults see. Consider a little boy who puts on lipstick and appears in the living room with a big smile, delighted to express his gender expression outside binary boxes. From his perspective, think of the difference in the following reactions. Scenario A: Daddy smiles back, gives his boy a hug, and exclaims, "You look beautiful." Scenario B: Daddy frowns, pushes his little boy away, and yells: "Go to your room right now, young man, and wipe that right off. Boys don't wear lipstick." In Scenario A, the little boy is mirrored back his own gender-bending self. In Scenario B, the little boy is mirrored back an image of himself as a boy who needs reprimanding and who needs to reflect his father's image rather than an image of himself. For every child, we would hope for Scenario A if we are committed to promoting gender health for all our children. And a reminder: Providing this positive gender mirror applies not just to parents but to every adult coming into contact with a child's gender creativity. We all have massive influence on the next generation's gender well-being.

In the beginning of life, little ones are highly dependent on their parents to be their mirror. As they get older, they do not have to rely on them as much. With greater independence and more sophisticated minds, if all goes well, they can start relying on their own internal mirrors—the picture they have an opportunity to draw of their gender self based on their own inner reflections, rather than feedback from others. They can become more cognizant of a discordance between what their internal mirror tells them about their gender self and what the outside world is mirroring back to them in distorted and negative ways. So, when Alx, a transgender boy, says, "They'll never understand how it feels to look at yourself in the mirror after being on hormones for a few months and you finally start seeing changes. Suddenly you're smiling at your appearance instead of hiding away," he may be revealing not just the experience of looking in an actual mirror. At a deeper level, he may be experiencing an arrival point in a long journey in which others around him heard what he was trying to say about himself, reinforced that self-image, and reflected back to him the boy who was there to be seen. And when L.W., a transgender girl, says, "I don't even want to think about having to go back to the dark place I was in before I was able to come out and access the care that my doctors have prescribed for me," she is not just referring to the shutdown of pediatric gender programs in her state. More poignantly, she may be imagining the distress of returning to a place where people, through distorted mirroring, would misgender her, particularly if she was denied the hormone treatment that had finally allowed her to be seen as the girl she knew herself to be.

Children Are Not Short Adults

As we listen to the voices and stories of these children, we are constantly reminded that children are rapidly moving organisms going from one stage of development to the next and not just short adults. Each country has its own "age of majority" when a young person is first recognized as an adult. On the other side are "minors," which is typically a word that kids, at least older kids, hate. But the truth of the matter is that life moves forward from birth to maturity and every culture has its own demarcation of childhood, how it rolls out, and what it means.

When it comes to children's gender selves, we are apt to make errors in opposite directions: Either we see no differences in the way children and adults live their gender, or we dismiss and discredit children's ability to know their gender—they are too young, too quickly changing, and haven't reached full brain development. To truly hear the children's voices and celebrate children's gender creativity in all its shapes and hues requires reminding ourselves that a two-year-old spinning their gender web will look very different than a seven-year-old, than an eleven-year-old compared to a fourteen-year-old, than a youth exiting adolescence. But in their own space and time, they can and do know their gender and how they want to express it.

At the same time, it's important to remember that children are not short adults—they aren't fully developed. Every child goes through critical stages of development before entering adulthood. Selma Fraiberg identified the preschool years, up until about age six, as "The Magic Years."[8] During this time, children embrace fantasy as a critical part of daily life. So—if a frog can turn into a prince, surely a boy can turn into a girl? Then, when children begin to enter the world of formal education, reality takes center stage and fantasy is firmly placed in the category of make-believe, while concrete thinking and the era of facts and figures sets in. In that period of life, a child begins to understand all the component parts of the gender web and how they matter—that we *do* have given bodies with certain body parts that are sex-typed, there are indeed social rules for how to do gender and structures to live within or beyond them. As children begin to roll out of those early years into puberty, enormous changes are occurring in their bodies, psyches, emotions, and in their growing independence that set the stage for the next era—adolescence. Parents shudder, educators scramble, youth set out, as we learned from the renowned psychologist Erik Erikson's influential work on the "eight stages of man,"[9] to discover and consolidate their identities and their future roles in the world.

Of course we cannot reduce the developmental progression from ages zero to eighteen into a paragraph. Yet, we believe that as we listen to a child, it's important to remind ourselves to adjust to their age or stage of childhood as we get their gender in focus and set out to learn about gender as the young ones are experiencing it. But one tenet remains constant throughout: No matter what age or stage, children are the arbiters of their own gender. We are simply their helpmates.

THE CHILDREN HAVE SPOKEN

Some years ago, I (Diane) and my colleague Colt St. Amand posed the question: "Why does a child have to change their name to authenticate their gender, why can't Susie just be a person's name rather than a girl's name, and why does someone have to grow breasts to claim their female self?"[10] In truth, it was a rhetorical question, but our best hope is that the voices and experiences of the children in this chapter have been able to answer that question. Sometimes a child may want to do all those things; sometimes they may feel compelled to do them to meet societal norms; sometimes they will feel free to do their own creative mix-and-match. However they put their own gender together, they draw from everything in them and around them to speak their gender, feel their gender, be their gender.

CHAPTER 7

What's a Parent to Do?

"We are blessed beyond comprehension to have a gender-nonconforming son. It's easy to feel blessed when you get what you expect. But can you feel that way and still be thankful when things turn out not as expected? . . . Yes, you can."
—Lori Duron, *Raising My Rainbow*

BEFORE OUR CHILDREN ARE EVER BORN, WE have dreams for them—we imagine what they'll look like, how they'll move and talk, who they will be someday. It's what Sigmund Freud once dubbed "expectable parental narcissism." It's the good kind of narcissism, the kind that binds us to the children we will be raising for many years, with all our hopes, wishes, and fears. In some cultures, children are seen as preformed beings; the only role of caregivers is to give birth to them and make sure they have all the nutrients to keep growing. In other cultures, newborns are thought of as empty slates, to be molded and shaped like soft clay by loving parental hands and community expectations, until they arrive at being the sturdy adults they will someday become.

The truth is neither one nor the other, but a combination of both: Nature and nurture account for the developmental unfolding of every child. Our children come to us already wired in certain ways, with a temperamental style that may have been recognizable even before they left the womb. One baby might make a ruckus in there, while the next one gently floats along in gentle waves. At the same time, parents have tremendous influence over how their children grow and who they will eventually become. Focusing in on gender, we can apply this to the gender web at work—the interweaving of nature, nurture, and culture. In this chapter we are going to grab hold of the nurture threads that belong to the parents.

Parents: Experts with Blind Spots

One of the most common mistakes mental health professionals can make in our work with children is to arrogantly dismiss parents as non-experts of their own child, relegating them instead to the status of interlopers who interfere with the good changes we are trying to make. I (Diane) can recall from my own postdoctoral training, reading the advice from Melanie Klein, one of the "mothers" (along with Anna Freud) of child psychoanalysis. The takeaway: Leave the parent at the consultation room door and get on with analyzing the child. Parents are simply the ones who caused the problem in the first place that only you can fix.

As you have probably discerned, neither of us abide by that tenet. We perceive parents as both leaders and fellow travelers in every child's journey from infancy to adulthood. And nothing could be truer of the gender journey. Aside from the medical professional who helps deliver a baby, parents are typically the first people a baby lays eyes on. Whether it is that person or someone else who becomes the caregiver, those adults who shepherd the baby through their childhood will know the ins and outs of that child's daily life and yearly growth like no one else.

And yet. While not specific to a child's evolving gender web but highlighted by it, is "parent as expert with blind spots." We see so much of our children and so much in them. At the same time, we have yet to meet a parent who has not been utterly astounded by something their child did, said, or felt at one time or another. This universal aspect of parenthood, "failing to see," likely contributed to the pseudo-diagnosis of "Rapid Onset Gender Dysphoria." Consider the scenario in which a young teen shows up in the family one day and communicates, for the very first time, that they are not the gender everyone thought they were, but rather something different—maybe it's transgender, nonbinary, genderqueer, agender, or maybe it's some unique, creative iteration of gender. For many parents, these comments are met with responses that range along the spectrum of "I never saw it coming" to "This cannot be," with accompanying feelings of shock, confusion, anxiety, or alarm.

Recognizing that parents can be experts of their child, we of course take those responses into consideration as we try to get a youth's authentic gender in focus. At the same time, we see the emotional support parents may need in those moments as their own foundation of gender is rocked to the core from the fallout following that experience we identified earlier—Rapid Onset Parental Discovery. A parent will think: What is this thing my child is trying to tell me that flies in the face of everything I have known about them? Keep in mind that any youth coming to their parents for the first time sharing a new status to their gender web may have already known it for months or years before revealing it to their parents, or to anyone but themselves. What we want to emphasize here is not what the child says or doesn't say, but the blow to parents that is caused by the surfacing of the potential blind spots when it comes to recognizing your child's gender.

It is not for us to say, but for the children to tell us their gender. Parents may wonder, "But how do we even know what they're saying?" It also raises another question: In a culture where gender has been perceived as a bedrock, can we trust ourselves to see what social shifts are there in the world of gender? Or is our gender vision blocked when we are confronted not by an abstract social concept, but by our own child as they navigate gender as infinite, multiple, or transformable rather than binary? Is it possible that parents are blinded by the internalization of the "immutable binary" based on what prenatal testing told them even before their baby was born?

Let us first give an example of the blind spots and then later address these two additional questions: 1) What psychological mechanisms prevent parents from recognizing their child's gender? 2) What support do parents need as their vision clears following the discovery that their own child's evolving gender web is either outside the binary or otherwise nonconforming to cultural standards?

Several years ago, I (Diane) was contacted by two parents who expressed concern about their teenage child, Andi, who had recently shared with their parents that they no longer identified as a girl and were wondering if they may be a trans boy. Andi's parents were in shock. They described a child who had always been the essence of "feminine" and to date had shown absolutely zero signs of acting, feeling, or looking like a boy. They asked if their child could come in for a session. I responded, "If she would like to meet with me, I'd be happy to talk to her. Do ask her." Their child very much wanted to meet with me.

The day of the appointment, I went to the waiting room to introduce myself to Andi, but there was only one young man waiting to be seen. So, I went back into my office to check my schedule to see if I might have made a scheduling error, but no, the hour was scheduled for Andi. I was the only person working in my office suite that day, so no one else was expected. I went back to the waiting room, and quietly asked if the young person was Andi. Upon the revelation that this was Andi, I introduced myself and invited Andi into my office.

Throughout the session, Andi easily opened up about gender explorations, questioning, and experimentation that they were trying. All the while, I had to quiet my own "gender noise" reverberating in my head: *However could these parents have missed what was right there to be seen—a youth who in every respect within our culture's norms was expressing themself as male—haircut, clothes, gait, mannerisms?* Andi helped me out of my gender fog and shared: "I've been looking like this for a long time. I don't know *how* my parents have missed it. Can you help?"

Andi's parents certainly missed it. But why? Let's go back to moments when a child is just a blip in our imagination. We're waiting to be a parent, sometimes impatiently. We imagine the child we'll have. Hundreds of those reveries are gendered. Anyone who has listened to the soundtrack of *Carousel* may remember Rodgers and Hammerstein's iconic song "Soliloquy" with the lyrics "My boy Bill, he'll be named after me." Billy Bigelow, the carnival barker, has just learned he's going to be a father. He belts out an aria about the boy he will have—"strong and tough as a tree," nobody's going to make a "sissy out of him." Suddenly his reverie about his boy Bill comes to a standstill as he asks himself—What if my boy Bill is a girl? It should be pointed out that Billy Bigelow, conceived by Rodgers and Hammerstein as a character in the 1940s, was absolutely not asking if his future child might turn out to be transgender. Instead, Billy's booming aria transforms into a gentle ballad about his visions of his future "pink and white" little girl in need of his protection and always coming home to Daddy.

Billy Bigelow was doing only what parents have done for generations—envisioning the child we are going to have, with the sex of the baby as a simple guiding light. Why else would gender reveal parties have taken off as they did? The belief of gender as a bedrock translates into gender coding our children before they are even born, with the proverbial question from the outside world (and within ourselves) about one codifier we feel we can count on—is it a boy or a girl? Why do we care so much? The reason may be found within the gender tropes of our own culture. It gives us a crystal ball in which we can picture our baby's future, from birth to adulthood. And when those futures are clearly delineated by boy versus girl, we are able to breathe a specific, visualized life into the child—the sweet and gentle child versus the strong and tough child.

Now, let's go back to Andi's parents. To them a baby girl was born. From then on, everything they saw in Andi was based on the implicit guidebook: Girls are like this, boys are like that. And they saw a little girl who in their vision stayed in her female lane, until that shocking day when Andi, now in high school, veered out of that lane by announcing, "I think I'm trans." I never bore witness to Andi's earlier childhood nor Andi's parents' gender observations as Andi grew. I did, however, listen to Andi's soulful teen narrative: "I cannot understand how they could not have seen it. I only wanted to play with boys. I was always trying on my brother's clothes. Are they blind or something?" Well, not blind, but maybe with blind spots. They certainly set me off-kilter as I searched in the waiting room for the girl who was not to be found, at least by gender presentation.

The takeaway here is that our codified sense of our child's gender—based on the sex recorded for them at birth and accompanied by our deeply internalized notions of immutable sex equates with immutable gender—is very hard to shake. And it is such organizing tropes of "gender for life" that can impair our vision of our own child, even with clear contrary evidence before us. For all of us, gender as moving boulders rather than as a bedrock can be seismic in effect. Taking it further, when it's not just a concept, but about the child you have raised, the initial moment of first learning that your child does not experience themself as the gender you always thought they were is beyond profound, sometimes earth-shattering. This destabilizing experience is never the end point but rather the beginning moment of a parent's own gender journey. It's a moment that calls for respect and compassion to facilitate parents' abilities to move forward. It's scary to feel that you've suddenly lost your footing, particularly when it comes to knowing your own child. There may be tears when it comes to leaving behind notions of gender as a foundation in the past, but there's now an opportunity, based on this new information imparted by your child, to develop a clearer vision of what is and what will be your child's journey forward.

As parents move forward, too, they will have to watch out for bandits along the road—the pundits and politicians disseminating misleading or false information—proclaiming gender is a craze with groomers and influencers luring young girls into trans cults; pontificating that doctors are pushing medications to irreversibly change their children's bodies when those children don't understand what's happening, and might even be as young as five years old; and insinuating that the gender-affirming clinics operate with no supporting scientific evidence. Conservative activists who have identified and then capitalized on the phenomenon of the swelling number of youth attesting to a trans or nonbinary gender identity recognize the confusion parents experience. Instead of helping parents out of their confusion, however, they make matters worse by playing on parents' fears and blind spots, infusing them with proffered ill-informed advice. Based on minimal to no professional expertise, these spokespeople direct parents to engage in actions already proved harmful to children and youth—guiding parents to save their children from getting swept up in this "transgender craze."

A mother of a youth who had been questioning their gender from a very young age and now, at the end of middle school, was wondering whether she might be a trans boy and might want testosterone, had this to say: "Our world is just being split in half by people who don't agree with each other—right and left. And now I know seven—*seven*—moms whose kids are saying they're transgender or nonbinary. All this has to be social media. It's causing all this. What else could it be?" Her thirteen-year-old was sitting right next to her as she said this. The youth looked like she had been hit by a ton of bricks. A mother is doubtful and confused; a gender-exploring young teen is stricken and scared.

Added to the mix is the often-expressed worry of parents who doubt the validity of their young teen's articulation of a gender expansive or transgender self because their child is suddenly over-emotional, obstinate, or disorganized, not at all like they used to be. The parents worry that the gender thing might be a part of an underlying mental illness. I (Diane) found a most helpful tongue-in-cheek response to parents in this situation: "Let us also consider a co-occurring diagnosis: Adolescence." Only then can we add on the potential contributor to the emotional tumult that often comes with transition from childhood to teendom: gender stress or distress, including the fear that parents will be blind to what their child is trying to say about their gender.

It's not easy to be either the child or the parent in this situation. Helping parents while also helping the child consistently proves to be the best recipe for better mental health for all involved.

Recovering from "I Never Saw It Coming"

When parents hear about Rapid Onset Gender Dysphoria and wonder if they are seeing it in their own child, they may initially feel unseen, unacknowledged, even maligned, and justifiably so. The process that parents are now embarking on can be challenging and also enriching, provided they get all the support they need.

Let's start with the research. Repeatedly, the research points in the same direction, starting with the work of Caitlin Ryan and her colleagues in the first years of the twenty-first century. Dr. Caitlin Ryan has been a pioneer and leader in the field of applied research related to LGBTQ+ youth and their mental health. She is the director of the Family Acceptance Project at the Marian Wright Edelman Institute at San Francisco State University, developed with her colleague Dr. Rafael Dìaz in 2002. They conducted the first comprehensive study of LGBTQ+ youth and their families and the first evidence-informed family support model to help diverse families learn to support their LGBTQ+ children, carving the path for many researchers to follow, such as members of the Pulse Project in Ontario and Dr. Sabra Katz-Wise and her research team at Harvard University/Boston Children's Hospital. The findings in these studies are straightforward and consistent: Children who receive support from their parents in weaving their individualized gender webs show better mental health outcomes. Children who do not receive support fare more poorly in terms of psychological well-being.[1]

But how do parents get to a place where they *can* be the providers of such support? Yes, if you want to support your child's gender exploration, listen, don't tell. But what happens if your ears are ringing from what you just heard? "Listen, don't tell" is simple in concept, but daunting in execution. The remedy? Keep listening, while also finding a safe space for yourself to work through your own thoughts and feelings—while protecting your child from what you think and feel, especially if those thoughts are negative. Parents need space to express those thoughts and feelings, no holds barred, either on their own, with a loved one, or with a professional who knows how to listen to the parents.

GRIEVING AND MOURNING

Often, after a child communicates to their parents, "I'm not the gender you thought I was," parents say that they are mourning the child they have lost, particularly when that articulation is followed by a full transition to a new gender. But the child is not dead, they're sitting right next to the parent on the couch. And that child predictably flinches when they hear their parents express that they have to mourn the child they've lost.

From the child's point of view, nothing was lost, instead something new was found. All that has changed is their gender pronouns, their name, how they look, or their self-description of their gender, and/or that they let their parents know or their parents found out on their own.

The parents, however, had codified and then formed bonds with a child they knew to be either a daughter or son, often from even before that child entered the world. From a parent's perspective, we can understand this poignant experience of mourning or grief as they adjust to their child's gender shift as a phenomenon that we call in our field "ambiguous loss." Ambiguous loss is a loss with no closure, as when a person has gone missing at sea or has been kidnapped and not yet found—a person who is gone, but not necessarily gone forever. In the case of the feelings about one's child, if that child should shift their gender self, it is the loss of the person who is at the same time right there. Perhaps we could reframe this loss as the disruption of a dream and the ending of a lived experience—in this case, one's life as the parent of a son or daughter changed to be that of the parent of a child who has discarded said gender.

The loss becomes even more heart-wrenching if the child asks or demands that all previous pictures of them in their previous gender iteration be packed away. Those images of their now perceived previous false gender self, reminders of an ill-fitting past, are now too upsetting to look at or have anyone else see. How painful it is for parents to take in the rejection of all the images they so carefully captured and displayed of the child they so loved and thought they knew inside and out, fueling that sense of loss and canceled memories.

Splitting hairs as to whether such feelings are grief, mourning, or ambiguous loss may simply be a matter of semantics. The most important piece to acknowledge is the loss of the dreams that the parents may have had for their child or the sense of surety of who that child was—our son, our daughter. Suddenly, someone threw the old gender GPS out the window and left the parent in the wilderness without even a simple compass. The more the child's gender comes as a surprise and the later in the child's life that the new gender iteration comes to light, the increased potential intensity of the loss and the need to find a guardrail to hang on to while finding new footing and a path forward. We can't emphasize enough how critical it is to make room for those feelings, while at the same time not getting caught in the weeds of confusion, shock, and/or sorrow.

Not all parents will experience such shock waves, especially if they've been aware of their child's gender creativity from early on and have gone through their own process of adjusting their gender lens. Yet, this early knowing does not exempt a parent from still having to readjust along the way if their child shifts their gender pathways or if external forces, such as the changing political field or gender bullying, get thrown in the path.

MY CHILD IS MAD AT ME. NOW WHAT?

Suppose you as a parent are taking all those steps to move forward in your gender journey with your child, and yet it does not seem to be working with said child. It can be horrifying to have your own child reject you or scream epithets about you being transphobic or a culprit in causing them gender minority stress. And that can happen. In addition to having to readjust the lens through which you see your child, you may also have to examine your own beliefs or implicit biases that blind or deafen you, or do a dirty trick of replacing the image your child is trying to convey about themself with your own fixed idea of who your child is and must be. It hurts your child. And when people are hurt, they are known to lash out. Children are particularly good at that. If such anger comes your way from your child, it is so important to keep in mind that underneath our children's wrath is often a cry for understanding and a fear of not being seen or heard, and most of all, a desire for your love.

It takes time, it takes patience, it takes feeling understood, but it does demand a shift in thinking and feeling if a child's gender health is to be ensured. Yes, it may be a far easier journey for the parent who has known since their child's earliest days that everyone got it wrong; the child is not the gender everyone thought they were. But even then, there may be emotional thorns along the way. The prickle of these emotional thorns can hurt even more if there is jousting with a co-parent who doesn't see their child's gender the same way, or with extended family members who raise difficult questions. And sometimes it can be yet another curveball coming directly from the child—that thing they told their parent about their gender isn't actually true anymore; maybe they're moving from nonbinary toward transgender, from transgender to no gender, or in any new direction that pulls the rug out from under the parent who is working hard to get their footing while erasing their blind spots.

And a word to the children: In the novel and streaming series, *Lessons in Chemistry*, Elizabeth Zott tells her 1950s TV audience at the end of each of her *Supper at Six* cooking shows, "Children, set the table. Your mother needs a moment to herself."[2] The same request applies to children as their parents adjust to new information about their child's gender. "Children, give your parents a moment to catch their breath. And then they can start moving."

Walking the Walk

In late 2023, journalist Emily Witt wrote an article in *The New Yorker* about a family with a transgender teen that beautifully illustrates the breadth and length the parental gender journey can take in putting feelings into action—walking the walk.[3] Witt tells the story of Kristen Chapman, a mother who lived in Tennessee with her husband and two children. Her older child, Willow, a teen, had come to know that she was a daughter, not the son her parents had thought based on her designated sex at birth. Willow had been receiving pediatric gender care in Tennessee, but when that care was banned in her state, Kristen realized it may be time to move to ensure Willow continued with the care to keep her healthy and affirmed in her gender.

Willow's father, Paul, had first questioned whether Willow could be old enough to decide about her gender at such a young age. Kristen pushed back, explaining to Paul that it was not their job as parents to unpack what Willow was communicating about who she was. Looking at their situation in a state that shut down any possibility of receiving gender-affirmative medical care for their child, they both agreed that in today's society, Willow would be safer for the rest of her life if she did not look male or endure the emergence of unwanted secondary sex characteristics like a beard or deep voice, and had the opportunity to have gender-affirming hormones to help her do that.

Help comes from unexpected sources. Paul, by talking to two trans women he knew—a coworker and a bartender at the pub he spent time at—was able to see his child better for who she was, rather than who he expected her to be. The bartender, not that much older than Willow, helped Paul understand that she still had scars on her arm from self-harm after her father rejected her for being trans. In the age-old adage that "love conquers all," Paul was never going to inflict such suffering on his child, and so he began to walk the walk.

Kristen had already started on her journey. While Paul remained behind with plans to join the family when financially feasible, Kristen relocated herself and her two children to Virginia, where she secured housing, schooling, a new community and job, and, most importantly of all, gender care for Willow. Soon after arriving in Virginia, Willow, who was able to access gender-affirming medical care, excitedly started a course of estrogen, none too soon as her prescription for the puberty blockers she had been taking was terminated in Tennessee when the ban had been put on pediatric gender care.

In Paul and Kristen's case, the walk was quite tangible. But for most parents, it will not necessitate a relocation to another state to ensure the gender health of their child, whatever that might be. The walk involves stepping beyond the phase of grief or loss (if it should occur), replacing your own dreams for your child with their visions of themselves, and coming forward as an ally and advocate for them, for your family, and for all the genders in your neighborhood.

Can Parents Teach Gender?

Children are universally known to be curious creatures. Typically, the first people they bring that curiosity to are their parents. Unfortunately, the imprint of adulthood seems to stomp out our curiosity if we let it. Any parent or caregiver can appreciate the constant barrage of "Why" questions—Why aren't stars purple? Why don't mommies wear pigtails? Where do the roses hide in winter? It may bring parents to the brink of distraction trying to answer all the "Whys," but we also celebrate the never-ending questions as children's constantly expanding wonder about how the world works in real and magical ways.

So, parents, be alerted—gender curiosity is no different than any other curiosity in a young child. If they see it or hear about it, they might want to know more about it, especially if it has personal meaning to them. This curiosity can begin as soon as a child learns to talk and has the cognitive ability to wonder. If a child is never exposed to new ideas or different ways of seeing the world, the child may never think to ask questions. On the other hand, if a child lives in a family or attends a school that talks about gender, or if they check things out online, parents will likely have a child who is curious to know more. The child who may be especially interested is the child who may already have something brewing inside about their own gender, just as the young child who cares about flowers will want to know where all the roses have gone.

No matter what your own child's gender journey may be, all children, when very young, come equipped with minds typically more flexible and creative than our own adult brains—that is, if we don't squelch their imaginations. Recall, in the young child's world, if a frog can become a prince, then anything is possible regarding transformation. It is, in Selma Fraiberg's words, the age of magical thinking, which also equates with expansive creativity, thus gender creativity. A parent can either close it down or feed that curiosity with sensitive responses.

As we write this, we hear the worried words of parents who object to exposing young children to ideas of sex and sexuality, and creating confusion in the children about their own gender. This fear or objection may bring a parent to pull a child from a school or demand books be removed from the library if they think the material their child would be exposed to will harm them. While absolutely respecting parents' desires to protect their children and shield them from harmful influences, we are calling on all parents to explore those fears so you can be the best gender teachers to your child in this twenty-first century world of gender creativity.

A gender creative child may be the person you're putting to bed every night, or the little person next to your child at their preschool. As we hope we've established, gender-diverse and transgender children do exist, some as young as two or three. It is hard to imagine how it would help to deny their existence. Parents can be a vital source in helping all children live with grace and acceptance in a gender-diverse world of little and big people.

Children, a new generation, are demonstrating a capacity to be far more flexible in their ability to recognize gender in all its splendor rather than limited to two boxes. But they still rely on feedback from their parents—either affirmation or refutation of their feelings, beliefs, and actions, about everything, including gender, whether their own or others'. As children grow and enter a larger world of school, neighborhood, and community, parents have a golden opportunity to discuss with their children what they are bringing back from that world regarding thoughts, feelings, and attitudes about gender. Maybe because another little boy wore a dress to school, they first get the idea that they can, too, after thinking it wasn't allowed. Then, sitting in the back seat of the car, they ask their dad about it on the drive home from school. In short, as children step into the bigger world, they get a window into how other people outside their family think about or "do" their gender. What they observe might match inner thoughts they were having about themselves and never knew how to put into words. And it might not.

As parents release their children into that outside world, they should always remember that the child's experiences out there regarding gender—theirs and others'—may be offering up words or images that they never had before. Who better than parents to step in as the most important arbiters of that information in early life and then critical influencers in later childhood, facilitating their child to feel confident in the gender web that is their own creation? Who could be more influential than a parent in teaching a child not just tolerance, but excitement about all the different gender webs that their friends are putting together for themselves? Always remember that the capacity for compassion to extend to people of all genders, like charity, begins at home. And that capacity depends on parents being optimal gender teachers to their children.

So, how do you become that gender teacher? By bringing in "gender literacy." For children, this means offering a lens to see gender in all its expansiveness and even to begin encouraging critical thinking skills, wondering about rigid gender rules—like "Why should only girls get to wear sparkly clothes?" or "Why are there boys' lines and girls' lines to go to recess? What if someone is both?" Such learning is a very relational experience for children. When young, they first look to their parents or caregivers as to whether their thoughts or feelings, either about themselves or others, are reflected back in a positive way. If the reflections are positive and encouraging, the child will feel free to explore more and express their true feelings. If the reflections back are disapproving, punitive, or restricting, the child learns to hide their true feelings or thoughts or put a stop to them because someone they depend on said they were not all right. Positive reflections and information about a gender expansive world are a sign of good teaching. Negative reflections and misinformation about the gender world we live in is poor teaching.

You may be wondering when this reflective teaching starts? It's not just listing the facts; it's about encouraging curiosity and critical thinking about gender, and it starts before a child is even born. All adults—and especially parents-to-be—have to do the work of unlearning whatever they may have absorbed that would count as restrictive notions of gender and replace it with a new gender literacy—which includes embracing gender in all the wonderful ways it may show up. It requires lifelong learning as history rolls forward with ever-evolving gender discoveries and shifts and as the next generation grows.

Learning can be transmitted to the children through our conscious efforts but also in our unconscious words and actions. Let's stay with conscious efforts. Here would be an example, one not just applicable to parents, but also to anyone in the position of teaching a child. If you are reading a book to your child and there is a page that does not send a good message about gender, you can stop and say, "Actually, I don't see it that way. I think it's OK for Johnny to wear nail polish if he wants to. What do you think?" As time goes on, you can have some Post-its nearby so that you and your child can be book editors—putting an editorial comment on the margins of the page or rewriting that part of the text to be more gender-inclusive if the text or illustrations are found to fall short.

Let us also learn from master educators that a vital part of teaching is learning from our students. We also have much to learn from our children. As we offer new vistas for the children to think about gender beyond two boxes and rigid gender rules, they in turn offer us their own visions of the world of gender. This reminds me (Diane) of my ten-year-old granddaughter's response when I told her that, when growing up in Chicago, the rule was that you had to wear a dress to school every day—rain, shine, hot, cold, or blizzard. My granddaughter was shocked and, having only experienced me as an outspoken feminist, burst out, incensed, "Grandma, why didn't you protest?!" Although not a parent but a parent-once-removed, it was a learning moment for me to step into the world of my granddaughter as she saw gender through the lens of a Generation Z child, unable to comprehend why we would ever put up with such a stupid gender rule. This afforded an opportunity for me not only to learn about the gender world from her twenty-first century grandchild's perspective but to then share with her the historical shifts that were not yet in place in the 1950s and early '60s.

From the mouths of babes comes material for the teaching curriculum of the parents as they generate new expanded notions of gender to their children. The children are living in a different gender world than the one we grew up in, and we have a lot to learn from them.

Calling All Parents

All children live with parents or caregivers, minus those older youth who have been forced to live on the streets after being thrown out of their homes because of their gender or sexual identity, or whatever other reason. Some of these parents may find themselves carrying a heavy load or traversing a thorny path as they raise their children while trying to make sense of gender's shifting terrain. Some may be the proudest parents you will ever meet. Some will have children as young as two crying out, "No, Daddy, me not boy. Me girl." Some will have older children coming home from school one day announcing, "By the way, my pronouns are now 'they/them.'" Some will have tweens seeming so happy before and suddenly collapsing at the threshold of puberty with gender stress pulsing through them. Some will have teens texting from the next room, "I'm trans and I want hormones NOW." Some will have children coming home from school sharing about a new girl in class—she used to be a boy but said everyone got it wrong and now her name is Madeline, which it should have been all along. Some will have children wanting to know why some people are mad at boys who wear dresses or girls who wear tuxedos. Some will have children getting teased because of their gender expressions. Some will have children just learning they are not allowed to read the book *First Year Out* at school or say the word "gay." Some will have their own parents expressing alarm or worry about the way they are letting the grandchildren stray from the girl/boy boxes of gender. Some will have children coming home confused: "How can someone be both a boy and a girl?"

Every one of these parents will be bombarded with opposing messages from the world around them—"Celebrate your child, let them be who they are, kudos for gender rainbows" versus "Beware the influencers and groomers with an agenda to turn your child trans, poison them with dangerous drugs, and even sterilize them, it's just a craze you must put a stop to." It's hard enough to walk the balance beam of raising a child to be the best person they can be while keeping them safe. Add gender and these opposing messages to the mix, just as more and more children are challenging their parents by exploring the gender new world, and we have parents who desperately need love, support, and accurate information rather than ideological riffs to have confidence in raising gender-healthy children.

"We are all God's children." Whether that is in your belief system or not, it directly translates to all children are our children. In a democratic, gender-inclusive world, our mandate is not only to raise our children as best we can, but to also watch over all the children in our community in need of nurturing, protection, and support. If every parent learns gender literacy, and then brings it to their children, and supports their schools in doing the same, we stand a good chance of generating healthy attitudes about gender. Parents can be relieved of the need to shield their children from the seismic shifts in evidence about gender. There's no need to cover their eyes. It is they who are pulling off their parents' blindfolds. Today's children may not have been around when girls in Chicago had to wear skirts to school in subzero temperatures, but they are right here as they correct Michelle (whom you will recall from the opening story of chapter 2) in her silliness of sending a little boy to the girls' bathroom just because he wears a dress. In their youthful exuberance, they absorb new gender more easily than their elders and then adeptly repurpose it to their own making.

In the book *Trans Kids: Being Gendered in the Twenty-First Century*, Dr. Tey Meadow gave every parent and child an invaluable gift by introducing the concept of "giving gender," which Dr. Meadow in turn attributed to the sociologist Janet Ward. What is "giving gender" exactly? Simply, a child depends on their parents to acknowledge, recognize, and make space for that child to be the gender they know themself to be at that specific cross-section of their life and express it in the way that feels the best fit. It is perhaps an extension of the feedback loop between parent and child when it comes to all of our children's gender journeys, no matter what path that journey takes. Since every child in our culture has the task of establishing a gender, every child will need their parents to "give" them gender in just these ways.

As we all know, giving comes in many different forms. As children typically get their first birthday gifts from their parents, so it is with gender, with the first gift coming in the form of the mirroring back to our children: the positive affirmation of who they are, how they want to dress, and things they want to do. But mirroring is not the only way parents "give" gender. Just as important is the messaging to the children that gender, like all other variations of human life, is something to be respected and acknowledged in all its shapes, colors, and hues, not just in two boxes, whether it's our own gender or someone else's.

Dr. Meadow offers a moving example of just how one parent "gave gender" to her child. Hunter, a six-year-old transgender boy, ran to his mother, Nan, exclaiming, "Mom, guess what? Did you know that Colton and Tommy both have *vaginas*?!" Nan could have answered in so many different ways. There could not be a better gift of giving gender than the way she did respond, simply saying, nonchalantly, "Sure honey . . . lots of boys have vaginas.'"[4]

This exchange between Nan and Hunter calls up many memories of reports from parents handling similar situations. Here's one: Marjorie, mother of six-year-old Daniel, wondered how she should answer when he came home confused, maybe even a little incensed about his friend at school: "Mommy, Jeremiah says he's a boy with a vagina. How could that be? That's impossible." How to answer? Marjorie's first inner response: "You're right. That's impossible." But then she caught herself and came up with this instead: "Well, yes, most boys have penises, but some boys have vaginas, and Jeremiah is one of the boys who has a vagina." This is an example of a parent "giving" gender to her child, a gift that might reverberate outward beyond Daniel to all his other friends at school as he reports back that yes, some boys have vaginas. If Daniel had come back later and asked, "Okay, so will Jeremiah never get a period because he's a boy now?," Marjorie might answer, "Jeremiah was born with a uterus and people who have a uterus get periods, whether they're a boy or a girl." Later on, Marjorie might add information about puberty blockers and gender-affirming hormones that help a boy with a uterus not to get periods or grow breasts. The important lesson is to give gender to a child, but make sure it's at a developmental level where they're ready to receive it.

So, a call to all parents: Give gender—whether at home, at school, at the workplace, everywhere. It is a good insurance policy for every child's gender health, no matter what gender pathway they take.

Getting to Work

We opened this chapter with the words of a parent, and we would like to do the same in closing. Laurie Frankel is an author and the mother of a transgender girl. In her novel, *This Is How It Always Is*, she offers a riveting fictional account of one family's journey with their transgender child and their other children. Yet it is the author's note at the end of the book that caught our eye with the realization that no one but a parent can truly speak for the experience of being one. We'd like to borrow her call to all of us regarding the twenty-first-century world of gender.

> I wish for my child, for all our children, a world where they can
> be who they are and become their most loved, blessed, appreciated
> selves. . . . For my child, for all our children, I want more options,
> more paths through the woods, wider ranges of normal, and
> unconditional love. Who *doesn't* want that?"[5]

Who indeed? So, children, give your parents a moment to catch their breath, and then make sure they get to work to give gender and make this genderful world happen.

CHAPTER 8

Gender Conundrums
Sports, Education, and Medicine

Unity, not uniformity, must be our aim.
We attain unity only through variety.
Differences must be integrated, not annihilated, not absorbed.
——Mary Parker Follett, social worker (1868–1933)

FISCHER, A THIRTEEN-YEAR-OLD TRANS GIRL, WAS NOT
particularly athletic or interested in sports. Her athletic accolades included a trophy for sportsmanship for her one season running cross
country. Then Fischer signed up to play field hockey because she
thought it would be fun. When there weren't enough team members,
she recruited friends and peers to fill the team. Within a month,
Fischer was ousted from the team she had helped pull together because the Kentucky High School Athletic Association's rules barred
transgender girls from playing on girls' sports teams unless they had
somehow completed sex reassignment, including genital surgeries if
after puberty. This is next to impossible under age eighteen in the
United States and most other countries.[1]

Fortunately, Fischer quickly rejoined the team after the school district ruled that their nondiscrimination clause shielded her from the
state's athletic regulation. She played the rest of the season. Her team
didn't win a single game, but Fischer didn't care about winning. She
played to have fun and for the mental health support that playing
on the team provided her. After the field hockey season ended, the
state of Kentucky passed the Fairness in Women's Sports Act in 2022,
which banned transgender girls from playing on girls' sports teams in
middle school, high school, and college—no exceptions. Fischer spoke

with the legislators before they voted on the bill. She told them, "I really don't want this bill to pass, because that means I can't play . . . and that will be extremely detrimental to my mental health, because it's a way to help me cope with things."[2] After the bill passed, legislators confirmed that Fischer was the only known transgender student playing on a girls' sports team in the entire state. For many people, it's not the numbers that count. Rather, it's the concern that other team members, cisgender females who have fought so hard for equal footing in competitive sports and especially if it is their daughters, would be outperformed by people with a constitutional physical advantage. In this chapter, we'll take a closer look at the controversy surrounding sports and education to understand why gender inclusivity is necessary and complicated. The second half of the chapter will consider factors, at times conflicting, when making decisions about gender-affirming medical care.

Trans Youth in Sports

Sports have always been strictly divided by sex and gender, so it is no wonder that transgender and nonbinary students playing on school sports teams is one of the more controversial gender topics. Even among those who say they support transgender rights in all other domains, there are many people who are in support of banning transgender girls in the name of protecting girls' sports. Those opposed to gender inclusion usually claim that designated male at birth students uniformly and necessarily have an athletic advantage over cisgender girls, regardless of the sport. Due to this athletic advantage, many people express fear and outrage that trans girls are taking opportunities away from cisgender girls, including the ability to excel in sports, win awards, and earn scholarships. Therefore, girls' sports must be protected from transgender girls who could take over and outperform their cisgender peers. Often, although not always, transgender boys are spared the same school sports bans because their sex designated at birth is female. Since female is considered the physically inferior sex, these athletes are not perceived to pose a danger to boys' sports teams or to cisgender boys' athletic opportunities.

Those in support of gender inclusion in sports point to the many benefits that sports provide to all students, such as increased self-esteem and a sense of belonging. These benefits are particularly important for transgender students who are more likely to contend with social and psychological stress due to discrimination, bullying, and many other factors. Supporters of gender inclusion also point to ways in which science supports inclusive polices and highlights negative impacts and risks of exclusive policies on transgender students, whether athletes or not.[3] Based on the research and our professional experiences with children and youth, we support transgender and gender-diverse students playing on the sports team that matches their gender identity, if this is their preference. However, we understand that this topic is quite complex, and it becomes even more complicated as children become teens, and teens become adults.

WHY ARE SCHOOL SPORTS IMPORTANT?

Regular physical activity improves bone health, cognitive function, muscular fitness, respiratory and cardiovascular health, mental health, and in particular, reduces depression and anxiety.[4] The ultimate focus of school sports (K–12) should be on health, wellness, and inclusion. We are talking about children and youth who want to play sports with their friends. And the trend has been that children's physical activity levels have steadily decreased over the decades. All children have the right to reap the physical benefits from school sports, but if a child is forced to play on a team that does not match their gender identity, they are essentially banned from sports and denied these potential benefits for many reasons. Playing sports on a team that matches one's sex designated at birth but not one's gender is likely to cause or exacerbate gender dysphoria, will betray a youth's privacy if they are not out as transgender, and is likely to undermine a sense of belonging and community. As Emet, a trans man and hockey field player describes, "Suppressing myself just to be able to play sports felt like a piece of me was dying, like I was killing myself at the same time—and that's why I ultimately came out and transitioned."[5]

Participation in youth sports also offers children opportunities to build self-esteem, discipline, and leadership skills, to practice teamwork, build community, and develop a sense of belonging, which supports their socioemotional development and psychological well-being. Rebekah, a sixteen-year-old trans girl, describes the following.

> In field hockey, you get to work on communication, looking for your teammates, and passing, and it's a lot of teamwork, which I really like ... It's exciting, it's fast, and we're all working toward a common goal. And we win together, we lose together ... I think the hardest part [of field hockey] is that I'm not very good at it. I exceed easily in the other aspects of my life. But in field hockey, I really have to try hard and work hard to get better. It taught me how to fall down and get back up and to know that being the worst on a team isn't bad. It gives me more room to grow ... And I think the most important thing is that sports give me a place that I know I'm not alone—I'm with my friends and my peers.[6]

Research on gender-inclusive sports policies shows significantly positive impacts on transgender and gender-diverse youth and has yet to find any negative impacts on cisgender students. For example, research shows the following in schools with gender-inclusive policies.

- LGBTQ+ athletes have nearly 20 percent lower rates of depressive symptoms.[7]

- Transgender and nonbinary athletes have higher grades than those who do not participate in sports.[8]

- Transgender and gender-diverse youth have a lower risk of suicide, greater feelings of safety, are less likely to experience victimization or harassment, and are less likely to skip class due to safety concerns when they attend schools with inclusive policies, whether or not they play sports.[9]

- Cisgender girls' participation in school sports either remained the same or increased after instating inclusive policies, such as in California, where cisgender girls' participation rose by approximately 14 percent in the six years following the enactment of gender-inclusive sports policies in 2014 (as opposed to a decrease in cisgender girls' sports participation in states with gender exclusive policies).[10]

Furthermore, research has found that transgender students in states with fully inclusive athletic policies were 14 percent less likely to have considered suicide than students in non-inclusive states.[11] Not only do gender-inclusive policies not cause harm to cisgender girls, but these policies clearly support the safety and mental health of transgender girls, an already vulnerable student population.

EXCLUSIVE POLICIES

Despite the clear benefits that athletics offer all children and particularly transgender youth, twenty-four US states banned transgender students from participating in school sports as of the writing of this book, with most states barring only transgender girls. Seventeen of these states enacted bans applicable from kindergarten through college,[12] meaning transgender and gender-diverse children as young as five years old are impacted. These gender-exclusive policies carry serious consequences, including significantly increased risk of poor mental health and sui-cidality among transgender students.[13] Furthermore, LGBTQ+ youth who attended schools with discriminatory policies had lower GPAs than other students, reported lower self-esteem, lower feelings of be-longing, higher rates of depression, and were three times as likely to have had school absences because they felt unsafe than those at schools with gender-inclusive policies.[14] While gender-inclusive policies show significant positive impacts on students, gender exclusive policies have harmful effects on transgender and gender-diverse children and youth.

In other parts of the world, such as in the UK, governments have not enacted the same kind of sweeping bans on transgender children and youth in sports that we see in the US. Instead, governmental guidance (as opposed to laws) is offered and varies depending on region. For example, the Department of Education in England guides schools and colleges to implement their own policies which prioritize safety and fairness, explicitly stating "allowing a gender questioning child to participate in sports with the opposite sex will not be appropriate if it risks safety or fairness."[15] While it is widely believed that these guidelines will be used to support policies based on exclusion, there is some room for schools to choose their own policies based on their student population. In Northern Ireland, the Education Authority similarly guides schools to consider safety and fairness, but their guidelines go a step further to discourage "blanket policies" and instead encourage that decisions are made on a case-by-case basis. The guidelines state, "It is important that the young person feels supported and that their best interests are promoted."[16]

UNFAIR ADVANTAGES

Exclusive policies are based on the belief that regardless of gender identity, DMAB youth have athletic advantages over DFAB youth even as young children. But do they? Research in the differences between male and female athletic abilities in prepubescent children is scarce. And when differences have appeared, it is difficult to determine if these differences are due to biology or the impact of social factors. For example, DMAB children are often socialized to be more physically active, which would then give them more practice in some of the skills tested in sports than DFAB children. Regardless, research does not consistently indicate significant athletic differences between sexes in young children. For example, the US Centers for Disease Control and Prevention (CDC) found no significant differences between core, lower, or upper body strength in male and female prepubescent children in a national review.[17]

If and when there are physical differences between male and female athletes, what can explain any biological advantages? Most people point to testosterone as the cause of physical changes that offer an edge in athletics, such as increased muscle mass and grip strength.

While testosterone has specific impacts on the body, cisgender girls also have testosterone to varying degrees, with some having higher amounts than others. One particularly notable example is the 10 percent of the designated female population worldwide who have polycystic ovarian syndrome (PCOS), which usually begins in puberty. PCOS can cause high testosterone levels that may result in masculinizing features, such as increased body hair, facial hair, and male-pattern baldness. Historically these cisgender female athletes have not been excluded from women's sports despite their potentially high levels of testosterone.[18] If participation in girls' and women's sports requires a specific testosterone level, would adolescent youth with PCOS need to take hormones (estrogen) to counteract the higher levels of testosterone and to qualify to play on girls' sports teams? And then what about the trans girls who have not started puberty and therefore don't yet have high levels of testosterone? Or those youth on puberty blockers and estrogen who likely have low levels of testosterone similar to their cisgender girl peers?

In light of what seems like such a logical idea—that testosterone offers athletic advantages—you might be surprised to learn that the role testosterone plays is unclear in the research. In fact, there is no documented science that consistently proves that testosterone necessarily offers athletic advantages. For example, testosterone may improve performance in some sports but not in others. Katrina Karkazis, an expert on testosterone and bioethics at Yale University explained, "Studies of testosterone levels in athletes do not show any clear, consistent relationship between testosterone and athletic performance. Sometimes testosterone is associated with better performance, but other studies show weak links or no links. And yet others show testosterone is associated with worse performance."[19]

Perhaps because science brings more questions than answers about gender and sex in sports, even the International Olympic Committee (IOC) made big changes to their policies regarding transgender athletes before the 2024 Olympics. The IOC announced that decisions were to be left to each individual sport's governing body, since each sport requires different skills and strengths. They further dictated that the governing bodies were now required to take additional contexts into consideration, such as ethical, legal, and mental health considerations beyond gender and physical appearance. This meant that determinations could no longer come down to just hormone levels, sex designated at birth, or surgeries in order to qualify for the team matching an athlete's gender identity.[20]

Given the small number of transgender athletes, best estimated to be about 1 percent of student athletes,[21] we think it's safe to say that transgender and gender-diverse students are not posing a significant threat to school sports or to cisgender girls. So far, research on gender inclusion in school sports has found no negative effects. To the contrary, research has demonstrated many positive effects for transgender and gender-diverse youth, including increased psychological well-being, lower suicide rates, improved academic performance, and decreased victimization and harassment.

So, what's the urgency to pass gender exclusive bans? It's certainly not rooted in science. Perhaps the urgency is not about protecting girls' sports, but because there is felt to be something dangerous about transgender children and youth, particularly trans girls.

Gender in the Classroom

Sports is only one facet of gender diversity in schools. Education is ripe with many controversial and complex issues related to gender, including the gender curriculum and classroom discussions, the availability of gender-neutral bathrooms, and which books are or are not on school library shelves. In the previous chapter, we looked at ways in which parents teach their children gender literacy, but now let's turn our attention to the importance of gender in the classroom. Schools (K–12) are the primary source for education, socialization, and learning culture (outside of families) for children and youth throughout much of the world. The education provided in public schools may at times be different than family lessons, beliefs, or experiences, which sometimes results in controversy surrounding what should and should not be discussed or taught in schools. Yet, schools are supposed to expose students to new ideas and support them in developing critical thinking skills.

I (Michelle) can remember as a child excitedly telling my dad he was wrong because, "My teacher said . . ." Outside of a few times when he simply said the teacher was wrong, my father used these opportunities to encourage me to slow down and weigh up the possibilities, to think for myself, and/or to seek further information so that I could potentially teach him and/or my teacher something new. This helped me to learn that I have a strong mind, that adults don't always know everything, and that sometimes there is not one "right" answer. It helps to build critical thinking skills that have proven so important in this current age of false and misleading information.

We hold a similar framework for teaching gender literacy: It is important to question if what you are taught about gender is correct or even logical, why things are the way they are, and to think about what gender means to you. For example, in one gender lesson, a teacher or parent may ask young children to list all the things that make girls and boys different, and then to reflect on the list to see if all the points actually make sense. Why does pink have to be a girl color? Why are all the toy police officers and firefighters boys? Even young preschoolers, such as the ones mentioned earlier in the book, who were very flexible about their ideas of gender, can often name gender stereotypes accurately even if they don't abide by them in real life. Therefore, this lesson offers early opportunities to consciously exercise critical thinking skills while also working to prevent the solidification of traditional gender stereotypes in the minds of children. This is important because traditional gender norms can be harmful and limiting to all people.

GENDER LESSONS

Children and youth need to feel accepted in their school community both for a sense of well-being and to promote learning. As Leif, a twenty-two-year-old transfemme described, "I went to school with my nails painted for the first time in second grade. And the whole class . . . I was like trying to cover them up and write so no one could see my nails. And my teacher leaned over and she told me, 'Boys paint their nails, too.' And it, like, literally meant the world to me."

One important way that children and youth come to feel accepted in their school community is to see themselves reflected back in role models, books, teachers, and school staff. Remember the psychological importance of mirroring that was explained in chapter 6? Children and youth need that from their communities as well as from their parents. This requires diversity of all types in schools and in the curriculum—gender, race, ethnicity, socioeconomic class, disability status, among many others. Unfortunately, there has been much controversy around this topic, with some US states moving to ban discussions of gender and/or books that discuss gender diversity or even have a gender-diverse character. The UK has no formal policies, but school librarians report a stiff increase in the number of requests to remove books with content about race, gender, or sexual identity, and more complaints coming from parents worried that their children are being exposed to books with such content. It is generally agreed that the controversies on such matters in the US are reaching across the Atlantic.[22] Most critiques of gender lessons in schools claim that this type of curriculum is politically motivated, biased toward left-leaning ideology, and runs the risk of making children transgender and/or confused about their own genders.

While we find these accusations to be baseless, perhaps more importantly, the opposition to teaching about gender in schools overlooks the fact that children are learning lessons about gender every day from the time they're born. The very first lessons come in the form of their sex-divided treatment as soon as they leave the womb, whether through the nursery room colors or how their cries are interpreted and responded to by parents.[23] As these little ones develop, they learn gender lessons through observation of their parents, siblings, and other family, household, and community members. These lessons continue to show up in preschools that have a girls' and boys' bathroom, anytime there is a division of toys and clothes by gender, or by observation that all their teachers are women, and the community's leaders or firefighters are all men. These lessons are further reinforced through praise and chastisement. "What a strong boy you are! No, you can't wear a dress!" "What a pretty girl you are! Let's sign you up for ballet, wrestling is far too rough." So, it is not so much that there is controversy around teaching children about gender because it's happening all the time. The real issue appears to be about what the lessons teach—whether traditional gender norms and stereotypes are reinforced, or whether gender diversity and inclusion are celebrated.

It is important for age-appropriate gender lessons to be taught in schools from the earliest years in order to create an inclusive environment that makes all children feel welcomed and teaches them to be themselves. This promotes healthy self-esteem and confidence, both of which support taking healthy risks in order to learn new things and can persist over a lifetime. Ensuring that the school curriculum attends to diversity, differences, and inclusion offers all children opportunities to see themselves and/or their families reflected so that their schools serve as an extension of their family and neighborhood communities.

Another significant reason for promoting inclusion and teaching about gender diversity in schools is to prevent bullying. As we discussed in chapter 5, transgender and gender-diverse children and youth are at much higher risks of being bullied and victimized than other youth. This is on top of all the other risk factors that these youth face, such as suicide, self-harm, depression, and anxiety. Feeling unsafe at school contributes to school absenteeism, poorer grades, and in some cases, dropping out altogether. To the contrary, teaching about gender in age-appropriate lessons helps all children feel welcomed and also decreases the likelihood of a child later bullying another student because of their gender identity or gender expression. After all, children are the most flexible, and they are usually not filled with hate until adults and/or life experiences teach them to hate.

An age-appropriate gender curriculum starting in the preschool years also offers parents and caregivers opportunities to learn how to support their child's gender health at each developmental stage, which all children need regardless of their gender identities. Important questions parents might want answered of their children include: How do I prevent my daughter from internalizing negative gender stereotypes, such as that math and science are "boy subjects"? Or how do I help my son express his emotions and not feel ashamed when he cries? How do I support my child when others misgender them? Therefore, it is important that schools (in addition to families) are working to dispel harmful gender stereotypes so that children of all genders know they can pursue any and all of their interests, grow up to be any kind of professional, and succeed at anything, regardless of their gender. This serves to remove barriers to learning and supports a more socially just world. There are people who feel that teaching gender literacy in schools is a violation of parental rights because some parents do not want their kids to learn about gender. Yet, protecting youth by withholding information about gender beyond two boxes and transgender lives in the age of the internet and social media is neither realistic nor protective. As we mentioned, teaching gender literacy supports students to think for themselves through building critical thinking skills. It is not about indoctrinating gender ideology.

What's Wrong with Gender-Affirming Medical Care?

Just as parents don't like school boards to determine whether their child can play sports, they don't want the government to make health care decisions for their children. Throughout this book, we have worked to clear up misinformation and cite research to demonstrate that gender-affirming care is evidence-based and why it is considered best practice in treatment for gender dysphoria around the globe. We want to reiterate that not all transgender and gender-diverse youth want or seek out gender-affirming medical care; many transgender people are happy with their bodies as they are or otherwise choose to not pursue this line of care. It is a misconception that Schuyler Bailar, the first openly trans man to compete in a NCAA Division I sport, explains perfectly, "Many people see medical transition as the only valid method of transition. Some will go so far as to claim that those who do not or do not want to medically transition are not actually transgender. This is inaccurate, transphobic, and cisnormative—assuming everyone must be cisgender and/or conform to cisgender expectations of body. *Transness is an identity, not an action*"[24] (emphasis added).

As reviewed in chapter 3, adolescents who want and are able to access gender-affirming medical care experience large improvements in their psychological well-being, dramatically reduced behavioral and emotional difficulties, depression and suicidal ideation, and suicide attempts. With this in mind, let's turn to how challenging decisions regarding gender-affirming medical care are made when left to families and providers, particularly when the answers are not always straightforward.

GENDER-AFFIRMING MEDICAL CARE IN PREPUBESCENT CHILDREN

As mentioned earlier in the book but bears repeating, there are *no* available gender-affirming medical interventions for transgender or gender-diverse children before they start puberty. Instead, gender-affirming care for prepubescent children may include therapeutic support for the child, the parents, and/or the family if needed, and education/advocacy around gender diversity in a child's school and community, if needed. The only gender transition available to prepubescent children is what is called a "social transition," which means the child shifts from one gender presentation to another and lives as a gender that feels most comfortable to them.

Social transition usually includes the use of different pronouns and/or name. It can include all the other ways a child might express their gender—their clothing, hair styles, accessories, and so on, although these expressions can often be experimented with even without a social transition. It can be a normal part of a child's gender journey to experiment with different names, pronouns, and gender expressions at home or in the company of known and trusted others while they are locating themselves in a gendered world. Yet, an actual public social transition usually occurs after a child has a stable sense of their gender and how they want to be recognized in the world. The reason for this is that a social transition can create anxiety for the child (and for adults). Remember that all change, even good change, often feels scary. But once settled in, we expect a child to present as more confident with themselves, more relaxed, and less anxious. If instead a child begins to appear more distressed, then their parents and providers need to investigate the cause, whether something was missed or misinterpreted, or if in the process of social transition, the child has discovered that their new gender presentation does not quite fit.

Some words of caution: A child's construction of their gender web is a continuous process, so if a social transition is rushed, it can foreclose a child's opportunity for identity exploration. We have seen this happen from the most well-meaning parents and caregivers. It can be difficult to sit in the unknown and ambiguity, especially if a child is urgently pressing for change and/or is in distress. We have certainly seen the three-year-old who demands a penis right now or the prepubescent fifth-grader who wants puberty blockers to preemptively prevent the slightest change in their body. Finding the right time and speed can be tricky—not wanting to go too fast, but also not wanting to slow down too much and stall the process.

When thinking about the process of social transition, it can be helpful to think about it as concentric circles starting in the center and moving outward. We start with the first small circle—immediate family. Then we gradually extend outward to larger circles—family friends, extended family, schools, community groups. Each path may look a little different depending on the context. A social transition is absolutely reversible, so the only real risk is if a child feels stuck afterward because they aren't given the freedom to change, even if it means transitioning genders again as they continue to discover more facets of themselves. Or if somehow a child's identity exploration is shut down. All of this may demand much from parents who are already holding a lot. They need to advocate on behalf of their child at school, with medical providers, extended family, neighbors, church communities, scout troops, soccer teams, and so on. This is when support from others, including schools, can be tremendously helpful in smoothing the transition.

WHAT ARE PUBERTY BLOCKERS AND ARE THEY SAFE?

Puberty blockers, scientifically known as gonadotropin-releasing hormone (GnRH) agonists, essentially put puberty on pause. This means that they pause or suppress the hormones that contribute to the body's physical changes during puberty. Puberty blockers have been safely used since 1981 to treat precocious puberty (i.e., breast development before age eight or testes growth before age nine). Over the years, many additional uses have been found for puberty blockers, such as in treatment for fertility issues, gynecological disorders, and hormone-sensitive cancers. Most controversially, they are and have been used to treat gender dysphoria in youth since they were first introduced for this purpose in the Netherlands in 1997. In the US, as of this writing, puberty blockers remain an off-label drug for pediatric gender care.

Off-label means that the drug was not created for this use and has not received FDA-approval, and many critics have used this as justification for denying puberty blockers to treat gender dysphoria in youth in the United States. This justification is misguided given that many drugs are prescribed for off-label uses. In fact, most of us have been prescribed medications used for off-label purposes. For example, beta blockers are FDA-approved to treat heart problems, diabetes, and hypertension. Yet, they are commonly prescribed off-label for fibromyalgia, generalized anxiety disorder, parkinsonian tremor, and atrial fibrillation. Generally speaking, there is no reason to pursue FDA-approval for drugs to treat their off-label uses because it would cost drug companies money to pursue, and it's unlikely to result in any increased sales. Simply put, there is no benefit for the drug company to do so.

The second issue noted by critics is the potential long-term adverse effects of puberty blockers, particularly with risk to bone density. We know from over forty years of use in treating precocious puberty that blockers do temporarily impact bone mineral density, but these children catch up to their peers by late adolescence. Therefore, puberty blockers are known to be generally safe when used to treat precocious puberty. The same is true in a gender-diverse child who takes puberty blockers and then decides to resume their endogenous puberty as opposed to going on to gender-affirming hormone treatment. Once a child stops the medication, their endogenous puberty resumes, and there have been no long-term adverse effects found in these children.[25]

Yet, the impact on bone density is less clear when puberty blockers are used on an ongoing basis to treat gender dysphoria. One study followed up with people who had been treated with puberty blockers before the age of eighteen, which were succeeded by at least nine years of gender-affirming hormone treatment. The study found that bone density did decline during GnRH treatment but caught up to pretreatment levels. The one exception was bone density in the lumbar spine of DMAB individuals in their late twenties.[26] Another study found that while puberty blockers may cause bone density loss, gender-affirming hormone treatment or hormones from endogenous puberty restores or, at least, improves bone density. It concludes that there are no negative long-term impacts for transgender people and that bone fractures are not more common in the transgender population.[27] So far, evidence suggests that the benefits of puberty blockers for transgender and gender-diverse youth far outweighs any side effects, and research continues to be ongoing.

The decision to provide a child with puberty blockers is attained through careful collaboration between a child, their parents, endocrinologists/pediatricians, and mental health providers. Puberty blockers can be started only once endogenous puberty (the puberty a child experiences without any medical intervention) has started, and puberty is creating or exacerbating gender dysphoria. Puberty blockers give transgender and gender-diverse youth and their families more time before having to make decisions that may include irreversible outcomes. For example, if a trans girl does not have access to puberty blockers and then to gender-affirming hormones, she will develop a deep voice and facial hair that will contribute to others seeing and treating her as a man. After a testosterone-based puberty, there is no way to change her voice other than through voice training, an Adam's apple would have to be removed surgically, and facial hair removed through electrolysis or other hair-removing procedures. This means that if young people who need puberty blockers are denied access, not only are there severe psychological risks, but it may result in the need for more surgeries and drastic measures down the road to align their physical bodies with who they know themselves to be internally.

GENDER-AFFIRMING HORMONE TREATMENT

As reviewed in chapter 3, when youth wanted and had access to gender-affirming hormone treatment—estrogen or testosterone—there were significant decreases in depression and suicidality, and these decreased symptoms continued well into adulthood. Prescriptions of estrogen or testosterone enable an individual to go through the puberty that aligns with their gender identity, or at least allows them to more closely align their physical bodies with their gender identity. Hormone-modulating medications have been used for a variety of health purposes over the years. Hormonal birth control is a great example, as is prescribing estrogen treatment after a hysterectomy or to treat symptoms of perimenopause. Similarly, testosterone has been used in cisgender men to alleviate symptoms of low testosterone levels, such as sexual dysfunction or mood changes. Hormone therapy, whether used for gender affirmation or for another use, does carry potential risks. Some possible side effects include blood clotting, high blood pressure, and liver inflammation. Genetic factors, other preexisting health conditions, and age, all impact an individual's risk level, so it's important that gender-affirming hormone therapy is monitored by a physician to minimize risks. Despite potential side effects, we continue to find that the benefits outweigh the risks.

WHAT EFFECTS DOES GENDER-AFFIRMING MEDICAL CARE HAVE ON FERTILITY?

Gender-affirming medical care can absolutely impact future fertility. The specific impacts are dependent on each person's particular medical path. For example, if a child takes puberty blockers and the decision is made to resume endogenous puberty, there is no impact on future fertility. If, however, a child starts puberty blockers at the onset of puberty, before the body has begun to produce mature gametes (eggs or sperm), and then goes directly to gender-affirming hormone treatment, this can cause infertility. Other pathways can impact fertility differently, such as starting gender-affirming hormone treatment after endogenous puberty. Regardless of the particular path, it is imperative that medical providers carefully and thoroughly explain the fertility risks to parents and youth. Furthermore, options for fertility preservation should be offered and explained.

For some youth, the process of fertility preservation can cause too much gender dysphoria, even to the point of significantly increased risks of suicidality and other mental health distress. In these cases, the conversation around alternatives to family building may be very important—possibilities of adoption, fertility treatments, surrogacy, foster families, blended families, and so on. This is where the mental health provider comes in as a member of the interdisciplinary team to have these very discussions with the child and family. Finally, all the benefits, potential risks, options, and timing must be carefully weighed in each individual case. In the simplest form, families and youth must consider the following with their providers.

- Blocking puberty can take away fertility options if the young person continues to receive gender-affirming hormone treatment.

- Going through endogenous puberty may protect future fertility.

- The experience of endogenous puberty and/or the irreversible changes of endogenous puberty can cause increased dysphoria and suicidality. Very few people become suicidal about medical infertility, but many do about gender dysphoria.

GENDER-AFFIRMING SURGERIES

Gender-affirming surgeries include a variety of possible procedures including "top" surgery (i.e., removal of breasts or breast enhancement), genital ("bottom") surgery (most commonly vaginoplasty or phalloplasty), reproductive surgeries (removal of ovaries or testes, hysterectomy), facial feminization surgery, jaw contouring surgery, or rhinoplasty. Gender-affirming surgeries are not commonly available to minors anywhere in the world. When minors have accessed gender-affirming surgery in the US, it has primarily been limited to top surgery (i.e., chest reconstruction/breast removal). While we do not have comprehensive stats on the number of minors who received gender-affirming surgeries in the US, one analysis on insurance claims found that 776 minors diagnosed with gender dysphoria had top surgery and fifty-six had genital surgeries from 2019 to 2021.[28] The review did not offer further specifics on what these surgeries entailed. Remember that regret after gender-affirming surgeries is much lower than in most other types of surgery and is only about 1 percent[29] compared to the 14 percent in the general population who regret other types of elective surgeries, such as knee replacement surgeries.[30]

Now that we have taken up many issues surrounding care for transgender and gender-diverse youth, let us now pull back to look within ourselves and our own experiences of gender.

CHAPTER 9

Through the Looking Glass

*I know full well that mixed in with unfamiliarity is a good
dose of prejudice, myth and misinformation that, as a cisgender
person, I've picked up over a lifetime. These are the ingredients
I have to work with. If I resist owning the prejudice I'm
carrying, I'm not only perpetuating it, I'm promoting it. This is
hard medicine to take, yet the cure is worth it.*
—Anna Bianchi, author of *Becoming an Ally to the Gender-Expansive
Child*, UK-based grandmother of a transgender child

WE HAVE BEEN ON A LONG JOURNEY together, and it is time
for a bit of rest and reflection. Some of our thoughts will be sugary
sweet, others like the hard medicine Anna Bianchi refers to in her
own journey forward. But, as she reassures us, it's all worth it. For the
children, for ourselves, for the community around us.

As psychologists from two generations, we hope we've done a good
enough job in establishing that gender is both internal and external—a
mixture of nature, nurture, and culture. Gender develops in a relational feedback loop between children and the adults supporting their
growth and development within a cultural context. As Diane posited
in her first book about gender—gender is born, gender is made.[1] In
this chapter, we want to focus on one element of the "made" part of
the equation. That would be the nurture side, or in other words, the
adult side of the child-adult feedback loop of gender. Let's point the
lens at the inner life of each of us who are now the nurturers of gender,
with an aim of peering through the looking glass to capture ways we
can reflect on and gain footing in this ever-evolving world of gender.

Haven't We Already Learned Enough?

Discoveries, knowledge, and new scientific findings about gender are never definitive; rather than a solid body of water, they resemble an ever-moving steam. That means that explaining gender will always be an open-ended process, in which we keep learning, stay curious, and remain just a little agnostic. I (Diane) had the honor of teaching courses on gender at the Osher Lifelong Learning Institute (OLLI) at the University of California, Berkeley, a program aimed at adults ages fifty and older, "with a passion for exploration, engagement and connection."[2] Among other activities, they have intergenerational exchanges and opportunities for members to connect and learn and grow together, with discovery of new knowledge and deeper ways of understanding the world and themselves. We're borrowing from OLLI's philosophy to establish a platform to keep on learning and growing in our discoveries about gender in cross-generational exchanges. It's important to keep building gender literacy at all ages—learning about gender in all its colors and varying hues and developing a critical eye toward gender tropes that could potentially compromise gender health.

We, as psychologists, continue to learn, too, and here is an example of our own growth from the first to the final pages of this book. We argued that the concept of "gender-neutral" makes a great deal of sense—dispense with rows of boy toys and girl toys, and just have "children's toys." Don't make girls' tool kits pink and boys' tool kits dark green to appeal to boys' and girls' gender preferences or conform to social expectations. Just mix it all up for all children without imposing such norms. But then a grandmother wrote to us, guiltily confessing that she lost her gender neutrality when she indulged her granddaughter with a sparkly tutu and glittery nail polish. This kicked off a memory from my (Diane's) early years as a mother. At five years old, my daughter announced that she would like to be a princess for Halloween. Intent on teaching my daughter about social responsibility and enlightened gender roles, I said, "Of course you can be a princess for Halloween. I'll be glad to sew your costume. And you will be a practical princess. You'll make your own bed, because practical princesses always make their own beds, you won't have servants, and you'll share the housework." I went on to sew her an elegant Audrey Hepburn–style A-line mauve satin dress, with a cone-shaped hat, chiffon cascading from its point. This was a bad move. All my daughter wanted was a Glinda-style puffy gown with layers and layers of tuille and a sequined bodice. My daughter has never forgiven me for that costume and rightfully so. Why? I wasn't mirroring my daughter for who she was, but who I wanted her to be, all the while thinking I was engaging in a good lesson. Years later, the practical princess story was critiqued by my daughter in her college essay "Growing up with a feminist mother," for which she earned an A+ to my failing grade. Lesson learned: Support a child for their gender as they want to express it, not how you think they should. This is the essence of the gender-affirmative model, and it applies as much to the little girl who resonates with all the cultural tropes about femininity as it does to the child who rebels against those same tropes.

As I responded to the grandmother who felt she had failed in "gender neutrality" by indulging her young granddaughter's delight in sparkles and frills, a new thought hit me like a ton of bricks. We shouldn't be aspiring to gender neutrality, but rather gender inclusivity. It's not "down with gender," but rather down with constricting gender *rules* and *regulations*. Anyone who is drawn to sparkles, frills, or tutus should be celebrated in their desires, just as Diane's daughter should have been celebrated in her desire for an over-the-top princess-arriving-at-the-ball costume, which admittedly, was probably a costume her younger brother would have been delighted by as well. This "enlightened" thought about gender inclusivity rather than gender neutrality is exactly what Diane shared with this grandmother, with a hope of alleviating her guilt and supporting her positive mirroring of her tutu-loving granddaughter.

Gender-affirmative practices and gender literacy require lifelong learning. For example, we have spoken freely about the "true gender self," the "authentic gender self," and "gender authenticity" over the years. We've also outlined the premise that gender is not necessarily fixed at any age but evolves over the course of a lifetime. We thought that wrapped it all up. Then, in 2023, Avgi Saketopoulou and Ann Pellegrini, two psychoanalytic authors with a wonderful understanding of gender beyond two boxes, published their book, *Gender Without Identity*. In it, they openly critiqued the concept of the true gender self or authentic gender self, understanding it as rooted in a fixed, deterministic, or "born that way" notion of gender. In their own words, they find problematic "those clinical approaches that treat non-normative gender or sexualities as fixed or a reflection of some internal 'truth,' because such approaches misunderstand that all gender/sexuality is an *unfolding and dynamic* psychic process, not a static or a predetermined one."[3]

We agree with the thoughts of these two authors as they have advanced our understanding of gender. We have learned so much from them. After closing the pages of their book, I (Diane) began to reflect on my own development of the term, adapted from D. W. Winnicott's work, of the "true gender self." My learning curve went like this: *Did I make a mistake? I never meant for the "true gender self" to signify an unwavering fixed gender self, but I must not have made it clear enough in my own writing. I always assumed that another term I made up, "gender creativity," would be recognized as a dynamic psychological process for the child over the course of childhood and beyond that may alter what is true or authentic for that particular child. And I thought I had made that crystal clear as I first laid out the concept of the "gender web."*

I found myself first becoming defensive, insisting within myself that I had always made it clear that "true" or "authentic" was never fixed in nature or static once discovered, but always embedded in both psychosocial context and internal discovery—and certainly subject to change over time.

I could have laid blame on the two authors, Saketopoulou and Pellegrini, for making me feel bad and misinterpreting key tenets of the gender-affirmative model that embraced the concept of gender authenticity. But I caught myself, and instead took a good look inside my own inner workings to explore, *Did I go wrong somewhere? Is there a part of me that unwittingly holds to some fixed notion of gender? What can I learn from Avgi and Ann, whose book I so appreciated? What can I do better?* The answer was simple: Go back and make sure we did a good enough job in this book in reflecting the wisdom gleaned from Avgi and Ann's book: Gender is real, gender can change; it is never fixed, it is never predetermined.

How do we more explicitly hold the dynamic unfolding of a child's gender web while also having language to describe their experience of their gender as ultimate truth? We will use this opportunity to demonstrate the need to keep learning about gender as we go and be open to our own gender blind spots or misconceptions—in this case, mine.

So, how can the link between the gender web and the discovery of the true gender self be best described on the basis of these reflections? Gender is an internal quest and discovery of a self that feels real and like the best fit. True gender is not static. Gender will be subject to alterations over time, with new truths replacing the old. Gender will shift as each person, from their earliest years to old age, engages in the inside processes of rediscovering their own gender based on changing bodies, maturing minds, new experiences within relational and social environments, and shifting cultural fields.

Perhaps it would be helpful to differentiate the "authenticity" of gender from the "authenticity" of an art piece. When it comes to the visual arts, if we're visiting a museum, we want to know if a piece is "authentically" a Picasso or a Renoir, for example, rather than a copy or a forgery. If we have the resources to purchase a piece of art, the purchase often comes with a certificate of authenticity, verifying that the work purchased was created by such and such artist, and no one else. The certificate of authenticity is not considered a pulsating, living document, but a permanent record to be attached to the art piece. There is no such certificate of authenticity for one's gender. All we can do is bring into focus the cross-section of our "authentic" or "true" gender self at any particular time, but gender is a canvas that can be painted over with different strokes across our life span, with no aspersion on its authenticity. The "truth" lies in the reality that the gender self is ours and no one else's. So, in this case, it's best to think of gender as a pulsating organism rather than a static painting. There's no need for a certificate of authenticity. Thank you to the authors of *Gender Without Identity* for providing me with a lifelong learning opportunity to stop, reflect, and correct what I had never realized I had not made clear about gender authenticity and the true gender self.

In each of the two examples above, the misguided Halloween costume and the fuzziness around true gender self, it required calling on internal processes—thoughts and feelings—to engage in lifelong gender learning. We now want to move to the most challenging work for all of us: Looking into ourselves to see how much our own internal messages get in the way and how much they allow us to be ambassadors, advocates, and allies for every child and every gender.

Locating Our Gender Ghosts and Gender Angels

We've established that if we want to learn about any child's gender, we need to listen, not tell. This task is easier said than done, but it is doable. If you want to know about anybody's gender, including your own, it's also important to stop and look inside yourself. I (Diane) recall the words "The Still Small Voice" written in raised letters across the cover of one of my childhood textbooks. As a child I loved that phrase and adapted it to my own idiosyncratic ways of thinking about internal messages related to my life and my experiences of it. I decided that these inner voices used an inside rather than outside voice, meaning they never yelled. The rule was that no matter how softly they spoke, it was really important to pay attention and listen to them. Hopefully, the still small voice would be sending out positive messages, but I had to be vigilant about the negative or nasty messages creeping in. I decided that my still small voice could either guide me forward or hold me back in doing "the right thing," whatever that might be in the moment.

When I grew up and began my own journey in studying gender, I called upon my earlier notions of the "still small voice" to better understand how gender thoughts reside within us. We can think of them as "still small gender whispers," sometimes barely audible, but always capable of coming across as firm and powerful. Some of these voices can be thought of as our gender-affirmative guiding light while others are anything but positive. In those latter instances, we might associate these still small gender whispers to what has become known as "implicit biases," defined as unconscious negative attitudes against a specific social group, which could definitely include gender. For example, implicit biases have been starkly revealed in experiments in which identical fictitious job applications are presented to research subjects, sometimes with a male applicant and sometimes with a female. You guessed it, the "man" got consistently higher ratings than the "woman," even when the raters consciously expressed beliefs in gender equality at the workplace. These implicit biases develop in the fast-thinking processes of the brain and require a shift to our slow thinking brains if we are to reject wrong assumptions and prejudices, and informatively choose our values and actions.

From still small gender whispers, Diane moved to the notion of gender angels and gender ghosts. Gender angels are those thoughts, feelings, and attitudes that reside within us, the lessons we've learned, efforts we've made to recognize gender in all its variations as a healthy part of being human. Gender angels allow you to promote gender health among youth. Gender angels facilitate gender acceptance within the entire milieu in which children live and are to be celebrated. But we also have gender ghosts lurking within us. These are the whispers we were all taught or absorbed that come together in beliefs, attitudes, feelings, and reactions that we may not even be aware of but that blind us from seeing gender in all its splendor. They might be governed by unconscious or implicit biases. They might include conscious messages like "Transgender boys are not 'real' males; transgender girls are not 'real' females," or "You can't just live in the middle and be both, it doesn't work that way" or "Weird, boys wearing nail polish," or "I refuse to use the pronoun 'they' in the singular. It's grammatically incorrect and just plain wrong."

Gender angels and gender ghosts are certainly influenced by outside sources, but ultimately, they live within us. Each of us will discover we have both gender angels and gender ghosts, whether we like it or not. Typically, gender angels and gender ghosts are in conflict with each other. But sometimes the conflict is so subterranean that we are not even aware there's a battle going on. Each of us is therefore assigned a task: To let the voices of the gender angels drown out the groanings of the gender ghosts. This means being vigilant about both your gender angels and your gender ghosts and allowing them all to come to the surface to be evaluated.

The aspiration, by our reckoning, is to let the gender angels be the victors over the gender ghosts. It's easier said than done. So, how do we do it? We can start by self-examination and self-reflection. Cast off being politically correct, and instead ask, for example, "Truthfully, how do I feel about boys wearing makeup or sparkly nail polish? Do I do a double take, feel a tightening in my stomach?" You might be thinking, "If implicit biases are unconscious, how do I even know I have them?" It's a good question, without an easy answer. We can borrow from our clinical work where we strive to make the unconscious conscious by providing safe spaces, empathetic listening, and open-ended, nonjudgmental curiosity in which a person can allow buried thoughts and feelings to rise to the surface to be examined. Having respectful feedback from others around you who you trust or hearing them share their own experiences can be a tremendous aid in bringing any of your gender ghosts to the light of day. It's also helpful to ask not only, "How do I feel about _____?" but also "How does what I feel about _____ affect others around me?" The "other" could be your own child, your child's classmate, a relative, a coworker, or just some hypothetical person. In this exercise, the center stage becomes not you but other people.

You might be asking, "But why should we engage in this battle between gender ghosts and gender angels?" There's a simple answer: Because anything else will cause harm to children of any gender, not to mention the families they live with, the schools they attend, the communities they reside in, and the culture at large.

We'd like to share an example of a layered story of gender angels being the victors. Many years ago, there was a family who attended a gender clinic. The caregivers were two foster parents of advanced age who were members of a conservative Christian denomination. The first gender ghost that appeared was actually one held collectively by the gender clinic's interdisciplinary team. In preparation for the foster parents and their eight-year-old foster child's first visit, the team braced themselves for what they projected to be a challenging appointment. The team envisioned that the older religious foster parents would be upset by their gender expansive young child who was insisting that everyone had gotten it wrong, that they were a girl, not the boy everyone thought they were. Implicit bias: Older white people of conservative religious beliefs will reject a transgender child and want that child "fixed" or purged of the sin of being transgender.

Nothing could have been further from the truth, although the family did have to wrestle with their own gender ghosts and call on their abundant gender angels to successfully be the victors. The foster mom, Linda Graves, took it upon herself to write up their family story to share with others, and we'd like to include some of her learning process. After hearing her child's insistent articulations that girl, not boy, was who the child was, Linda began to educate herself about transgender children, slowly coming to the realization that this was what they were dealing with. When she learned that about 41 percent of these children and youth attempted or completed a suicide, she scrutinized her own beliefs about children and gender and realized that she could not let her foster child be one of those kids. In her own words: "We had to embrace him for who he is and not let our fear or pride get in the way of him becoming a whole person."

Over time, she and her husband educated themselves, attended support groups, and helped their child socially transition, not without a great deal of fear on their parts. Their fear, generated by the dangers presented to transgender children and the judgement placed on the parents, would have also been fed by implicit biases or explicit messages from their church elders about the "sin" of being transgender. As

Linda put it, she was not worried about the other children, who she felt would be accepting and understanding (governed by their own gender angels), but rather the gender ghosts residing within the adults in their community: "I'm afraid it's the adults that feel strongly about things they don't understand."

Yet Linda and her husband's own gender angels were fortified by their child's school principal when their foster child returned to school as a girl. The principal informed Linda that she and her husband had offered a special prayer for the child, praying that everything would go well with the social transition. In Linda's own words, "Just to know that other Christians were there for us and cared enough to pray for my child. That was a real blessing!" If that is not literally a gender angel, we don't know what else could be.

Linda's story came to a close with these words: "I'm writing this, because I'm sure some think we have lost our minds or are very wrong for letting our child present as a different gender from that which she was born with. I feel that C. is a SPECIAL gift from God!"[4] With blessings and her strong belief in God's special gift, Linda and her husband indeed let their gender angels drown out any moans or groans from gender ghosts. Observing the parents' strength, resilience, and gender acceptance also encouraged the clinic team to do a close examination of their own gender ghosts, so as to never malign a family based on biased cultural assumptions absent of any information about their actual responses to their child's gender expansiveness.

So, the lifelong learning lesson is this: To make a better world for people of all genders, we have to first bring to light both our gender ghosts and our gender angels, with no criticism of our character for having gender ghosts, because we all have them. Then we have to engage in a bit of warfare in which we let the gender angels conquer the gender ghosts. Put in more peace-oriented terms, we have to reflect on our own inner gender messages—consider how they might be communicated, wittingly or unwittingly, to those around us, and learn what we want to keep and those we want to discard as we go. Our best tool in doing this is the dual processing system. We call on both our fast, intuitive thinking and our slow, more rational thinking. Some people think of this as left brain (rational) and right brain (intuitive) thinking. Whatever paradigm works best for us, the task is the same. Let all our thoughts and feelings come to the surface for reflection and resolution.

Calling On Our Own Gender Creativity

We have introduced the concept of "gender creativity": how each child applies their own inner resources, nurtured by the people around them, to spin their own unique gender web based on the myriad of nature, nurture, and culture threads, with no two ever being exactly the same. We've also learned that nurturing a child's gender creativity calls on being gender creative ourselves.

Here is an example: Some children know from a very early age that their gender does not match the sex recorded for them at birth. Some of these children identify as transgender girls, some as transgender boys. As they grow older, they become more cognizant of the limitations of their body that code them as either "male" or "female" in our culture. Cisgender girls get periods when they go through puberty, whereas trans girls never do. Cisgender girls begin to grow breasts as they enter puberty. Transgender girls may have to wait until they can be considered for gender-affirming hormones (estrogen) to grow breasts. In the meantime, they begin to watch all their girlfriends begin to wear bras while they endure a flat chest. This can cause a lot of sadness or distress for the transgender girl arriving at the age when all her female peers are starting puberty, and she finds herself in the undesirable category of "late bloomer." Having no breast development in contrast to her peers may generate additional anxiety if she has chosen not to share with others her recorded sex at birth; she may fret that she now has a target on her back revealing to others that she is not just a girl, but a trans girl.

You're probably wondering: Okay, so what does this have to do with adult gender creativity? Here we go. Alexandra was such a girl.

Alexandra's therapist worked with her to imagine how she could feel comfortable with her peers. Alexandra's first response: "Let me start estrogen so I can grow breasts." It was not a possibility, since Alexandra had not started puberty yet and, even if she had, by her gender clinic's protocols, given her young age, she would have been eligible only for puberty blockers, not gender-affirming hormones. Alexandra became distraught, not wanting to hear that estrogen wasn't a possibility at that time, and kept insisting, "Why not?" After recovering from the disappointment, Alexandra reported that she, with her mother's help, had purchased a bra, but she had no breasts to fill it. The therapist offered the possibility of a bra with breast inserts, having been educated by older trans girls in their own affirmations of their female identity. Alexandra's face lit up, and again with her mother's support, purchased breast inserts. But the inserts, even the smallest size, were too big for Alexandra. Her good mood deflated. So, she and her therapist came up with a new solution—the filling used for pillows or stuffed animals that she could mold to fit her own body. Alexandra liked to sew and once again her face brightened with this new idea and off she went to design her own inserts. Alexandra now felt ecstatic about her creative ways of feeling happy among her peers with her "budding breasts" visible under her shirt, just like her friends.

Here comes the moment when a person takes a stab at their own gender creativity, often after bearing witness to a child exercising it themselves. For this therapist, she met her young patient's gender creativity that took the form of fashioning breasts when there were none. After this session, the therapist rested in her chair, left with her own ruminations: Was she encouraging artifice, "untruths," and denial of reality by offering her own creative solutions to Alexandra's flat-chest-dysphoria? Or was she simply offering her own gender creativity for Alexandra to use as needed to reduce gender angst and bolster gender comfort? We'll leave it to you as readers to decide the answer, but this example suffices as an illustration of one therapist's endeavors to exercise her own gender creativity with a gender creative child.

Now, consider your own gender development and your own gender creativity along the way. Ask yourself how you remember your own gender journey, recalling that every person has one, and no two individuals' journeys are the same. Have you ever felt like a "gender outlaw" breaking the rules that were set out for you for the "right way" to do gender—buying a piece of clothing from the "wrong" section of the department store, taking a job typically coded for the gender you are not, and so on? You may discover quite a bit about your own gender creativity through these mental exercises. Gender creativity is not only about how we put our own gender together. It is also our capacity to creatively understand other people's gender and each of their unique gender webs. Here's a helpful prompt to check in with yourself about your own gender creativity and its extension to others: What would you have done or what *did* you do if someone told you that you couldn't be the gender you knew yourself to be, or told you that you couldn't do certain things because of the gender you are? How would that feel or how *did* that feel? We have found that this very query and the subsequent explorations have proved to be some of the most powerful catalysts in becoming aware of and enhancing our own gender creativity, which in turn will contribute to our collective responsibility as gender teachers.

Going Forth

Lifelong learning involves absorbing. Exploring our gender angels and gender ghosts involves culling from the inside, introducing a whole new function of the gender mirror and gender mirroring. Rather than becoming the mirror for a child, reflecting back to them as accurately as you can what they are showing and telling you about their gender self, this time the mirror is facing you. We might think of it as a gender selfie. It requires taking a good hard look at ourselves in the mirror, with all our beauty and all our flaws. It involves going beyond the reflective surface and climbing through the looking glass to do a deep examination of our inner life.

There are never shortcuts to examining our own thoughts and be-liefs, but here is a brief ten-item "cheat sheet" to get everyone on their way.

- Overcoming gender biases or transphobia within ourselves involves reminding ourselves that subtle actions can cause significant harm (known as microaggressions).

- Discovering gender ghosts residing within us does not equate with being a bad person, just a person who has been affected by the messages infiltrating from the outside world.

- Taking time for self-reflection and self-examination is the best insurance policy against the domination of gender ghosts.

- Gender angels are "uppers"; gender ghosts are "downers."

- People are not islands: Gender acceptance is embedded in connection and community, including sometimes critical feedback from others about deficits in your own gender literacy or when your gender ghosts seem to be surfacing or taking over.

- Since every person has a gender, ask yourself how you put yours together (who you are and how you express yourself)—when you were a child, growing up, and now—and how it has changed over time.

- If you are a parent, remind yourself that when it comes to your child's gender, at the root it is not about your dreams for your child, but your child's dreams for themselves.

- Keep brushing up on your gender literacy.

- Call on your own gender creativity.

- As lifelong learners, keep listening to the children as our gender mentors, and catch yourself from saying, "They're not old enough to know who they are."

We have come to see the need for all of us to be "good gender citizens," translated to being strong advocates, ambassadors, and allies for children of all genders, not to mention for adults of all genders as well. As good citizens, it is our responsibility to tend not just to our own or our children's genders, but to all people's genders, all of which relies on taking a good look inside ourselves. We must also hold in mind that gender advocates, ambassadors, and allies need care as well, which means we're all taking care of each other.

Let us take a moment to reflect on ourselves as gender teachers, not just lifelong learners. On our own gender journey, the most common mistakes we may make are as teachers. If we teach children that only girls can wear sparkly clothes, we teach them to condemn the boy who loves sparkly things. If we teach children that girls should stay home and be mothers and boys should find a job to support their families, we have just decimated the hopes and dreams for a world in which people can be who they are and do what they want to do, regardless of their gender. Good teaching circles back to gender literacy with its helpmate, self-reflection.

We hope that by explaining gender as we see it you will in turn be able to explain gender to others, having done your own self-reflection and responded to the invitation to commit yourself to lifelong learning to keep abreast of gender literacy as times change and more information comes to light. Ongoing research exists and is expanding each day, informing us that the outlook for transgender and gender diverse children looks good, as long as they receive all the support they need. The ability to think critically about gender, to absorb the new paradigm of gender infinity rather than remain confined to two boxes, and recognize the need to spread what you have learned to others might be compared to what others before us have successfully done to increase reading literacy around the world.

As we engage in these efforts, can we possibly anticipate what's coming up next in the gender world of the twenty-first century? We'd like to conclude by taking a stab at it before we say adieu.

CHAPTER 10

Gender Evolution to Revolution
What's Next?

Let us remain vigilant against rigid ideological positions that often, under the guise of good intentions, separate us from reality and prevent us from moving forward.
—Pope Francis, Christmas greetings
to the Curia, December 21, 2023

POPE FRANCIS'S WORDS CAN GUIDE US IN acknowledging the realities in this gender new world and dispensing with rigid ideological positions, no matter what your religious or cultural affiliations. It's now our job to go forward as advocates, ambassadors, and allies for children of all genders. As Maya Angelou said, "When you know better, you do better," and we could think of no truer message as we move forward—stay gender inquisitive, not gender ideological, and put knowledge to good use.

Earlier the same week that Pope Francis delivered these greetings to the Curia, he also announced an ordinance that directs the Catholic church to give blessings to same-sex couples. It took ten years of deliberation and many discussions with the LGBT members of the church, accompanied by objections from more conservative members, for Pope Francis to arrive at blessing these unions. And he did this by listening, over and over again.[1]

Pope Francis's 2023 papal doctrine on blessing same-sex couples is still a far cry from honoring marriages between people of all sexual identities, with the church still maintaining that the institution of marriage applies only to a man and a woman. Of course, we wish that he had taken the bigger step to recognize and honor same-sex marriages in the spirit of marriage equality. We could have also wished that he would have taken the opportunity to declare all LGBTQ+ people as paragons of goodness rather than sinners in need of repentance. Nonetheless, given the Vatican's traditional rejection toward anyone other than cisgender, heterosexual people, his declarations are a testimonial to the possibility of forward movement throughout the world if we keep working at it, keep learning, keep teaching, and do our best to ensure that we move forward to promote gender health. To remind us of the benefits of keeping at it, we thank you, Pope Francis.

As we draw *Gender Explained* to a close, our greatest hope is that we have done a good enough job in bringing you along on our journey to explain gender in the present. We reviewed how the youngest generations have opened up gender so that it now comes in more than two boxes, and each person develops their own unique gender created from all the sources—nature, nurture, and culture—and this is all impacted by the passage of time. We examined all the anxiety surrounding gender in our society today and how this anxiety manifests and impacts children and youth. We listened to the voices of youth themselves and explored the journeys of a few parents. We've taken up controversial issues in order to replace belief-driven false information with evidence-based scientific research. We've advocated for transgender and gender-diverse children and youth to have access to all that they need to thrive. Now we come to the final step in this exciting journey and ask—What comes next? How can all of us be part of moving forward to secure gender health for all who have a gender? And we do mean *all*.

Past, Present, and Future Tense

Let us not forget that there is no future without either a present or a past. We've spent a lot of time focusing on gender in the present, but now let us tell you the story of a three-year-old girl and her brother that might give us a window into where gender is headed in the future. This child was designated female at birth, has no doubt in her mind that she is a girl, lover of sparkles and anything pink or frilly, and is all about princesses in fairytales. She and her five-year-old brother, who is all about trucks and mechanical moving parts, both talk about friends who are "they." These two children will ask of a stuffed animal, "Is it she, he, or they?" There is a good chance that someone has read them the 2021 children's book, *What Are Your Words? A Book About Pronouns*, where the main character Ari struggles to figure out what gender pronouns fit best, is offered all kinds of possibilities, and finally announces, "*they* and *them* feel right today."[2] For these three- and five-year old siblings, binary boxes are a thing of the past.

Thinking toward the future, "they" in the singular has become such a part of the discourse among English speakers that, at the close of 2023, *The New York Times* published a piece "Knowing When 'They' Means One" offering strategies to know when "they" refers to one person rather than many. The piece goes on to remind us that the Oxford English Dictionary and Merriam-Webster have declared "they" used in the singular to be acceptable.[3] It's not that nonbinary folks would have desisted in adopting the singular "they" pronoun to communicate their gender without the approval of the English language overseers, but the point is to document that history is indeed rolling forward when it comes to gender, how we all express it, and the expanded language used to capture it. We expect language will continue to evolve in order to more accurately capture experiences, and in turn, that the expanded vocabulary may offer greater understandings of oneself and others.

We have tried our best to demonstrate that gender beyond two boxes did not just fall from the sky or erupt from the earth's epicenter in some sudden explosion in the twenty-first century. Diane, in a research exploration many years ago, could locate no culture anthropologically or historically that did not have gender as an organizing feature, albeit varying significantly from culture to culture. So, we have concluded that gender, in some iteration or another, is a concept and organizing structure of human life that is here to stay, although it will continue to move, pulsate, and transform itself as time goes by. Sometimes it will even circle back to where it has been before.

Speaking of the past, the North Hertfordshire Museum in the UK determined in 2023 that the Roman Emperor Elagabalus, who ruled from 218 to 222 CE, was actually a transgender woman after a review of classical texts. The museum staff announced that going forward, Elagabalus would be referred to with the pronouns she/her. Those ancient texts alleged that Elagabalus had once said, "Call me not Lord, for I am a Lady" and had also asked whether there was a surgical procedure that could make them a woman. Of course, controversy has ensued as people try to make sense of the past through a present-day lens. While an executive member of the council that runs the museum stated, "We know that Elagabalus identified as a woman and was explicit about which pronouns to use, which shows that pronouns are not a new thing," critics of the museum's decision have raised doubts.

Detractors point out that Elagabalus was just a young teenager when they (we're going gender-neutral here) expressed those sentiments about their gender (remember: is it just a phase or a transgender craze?). Perhaps the recordings of Elagabalus's gender articulations and descriptions of their gender expressions (wearing makeup, shaving body hair, donning wigs) were proffered during Elagabalus's reign, in an attempt to attack the adolescent's character and ability to reign as emperor. Mary Beard, author of *Emperor of Rome: Ruling the Ancient Roman World*, could have been directing her comments specifically to us, writers and readers of *Gender Explained*, when she commented on the controversy surrounding this young emperor as a she/her or a he/him: "This is as tricky [an] area in the ancient world as it is now. What is said by Romans about Elagabalus powerfully reminds us that debates about the boundaries between male and female go back thousands of years (we are not the first generation to have those debates)."[4] So, too, this is not the first era of gender debaters, and this most certainly will not be the last, but having these debates, we do think we are emerging from a liminal space between gender laid out in two boxes and gender stretching out to infinity.

Are We Crossing a Gender Threshold?

"Liminal" derives from the Latin word "threshold." Liminal space is defined as the actual space or time in which you shift from one phase to another. Historical examples of liminal space include when people first learned that the earth was round rather than flat; when scribes were replaced with printing presses; when industrial machines reduced the need for manual labor; when computers replaced typewriters; and most recently, when Artificial Intelligence (AI) appears to be overtaking the human brain. What all these historical examples have in common is the fear experienced by so many people that civilization was about to go to hell in a handbasket—until they adjusted to the change.

And the change was never at rapid speed. It was established in the third century AD that the earth was round, but it took until the fifteenth century for people to commonly accept it. In the fifteenth century, after the printing of the Gutenberg Bible, it was argued that the printing press would never last and that handwritten paper manuscripts were morally superior to mechanically produced documents. It took more than a few centuries to overcome that sentiment. During the industrial revolution in the early nineteenth century, a group of English workers called Luddites made their mark by attacking factories and destroying machinery as a means of protest against the destruction of the cottage textile industry in which cloth had been made by hand. To this day, we still have Luddites: people who are opposed to technological change.

So, let's review. In the twenty-first century, it is now commonly accepted that the earth is round; very few people opt for a handwritten text over a mass-produced book or prefer a manual typewriter over a computer to write a document. People have accepted an automated society. Artificial intelligence—the jury's out on that one, but nobody seems to be fleeing from ChatGPT or Copilot.

Now, throw gender into the mix: Gender in all its combinations and permutations is replacing gender in two boxes with its rigid rules and regulations. Not just in the US, but everywhere. Are we caught in a liminal space, or have we already crossed the threshold with no turning back? Time will tell, but in learning from the past and clarifying the present, when we project into the future, all signs point in the direction of a gender evolution that is now crystallizing into a more radical gender revolution. The revolution is led by the children—the next generation—with the adults sometimes chasing behind. We appear to have a revolution that makes some people so anxious that they can't even think straight, such as when someone truly believes that trans women are men posing as women to rape other women in the restroom. As reviewed earlier, it is part of the human condition to be wary of wide-sweeping changes. Yet given time, people adjust, and change prevails. That is exactly what we see happening with gender.

Gender Change Makers

John Lewis, the famous civil rights leader and Georgia congressman, called on all of us to make good trouble to save our country and preserve democracy. Good trouble, which might involve civil disobedience, was necessary to both fight for social justice and inspire social change.[5] Congressman Lewis died in 2020 but left us with a legacy that we can easily apply to ensuring gender justice. Imagining good trouble comes in handy as we plough through a time of great controversy between preserving gender as we've known it—something that comes in two distinct boxes determined at birth—and embracing new concepts of gender, ones that go beyond those two boxes to acknowledging gender in all its expansive multiplicity. In the present day and age, if you stand for the latter, you might find yourself making good trouble.

Many ways come to mind of making good trouble to promote the human right to live in the gender that is the best fit, free from aspersion and bolstered by acceptance. But we think one local effort will suffice to illuminate where gender is headed with good trouble to guide it. In November 2023, a school district in the conservative town of Sherman, Texas, halted a high school production of *Oklahoma!* after a transgender boy was cast in a lead male role. School administrators made a unilateral decision that the school would cast only students designated female at birth in female roles and students designated male at birth in male roles, which they communicated to students' parents. Shakespeare might be turning in his grave, because in his time only those designated male at birth were allowed on stage in both male *and* female roles. But back to Sherman, Texas, in 2023. As the result of this new school policy, several transgender and nonbinary students lost their parts, along with cisgender girls who had been cast in male roles. To the general public, the district reported that the problem with the play was the inappropriate content of this 1943 musical (sexual and profane). Back at the school, the theater teacher who objected to the decision was escorted out by the principal, and the set for the musical that took two months for the students to build was torn down.

The story does not end there, however, because here comes the good trouble. Students and outraged parents protested, and the student performers rejected the school's offer to instead put on a version of *Oklahoma!* revamped for middle schoolers or younger folks with no solos and with added non-human roles as cattle and birds. Theater actors, faculty, and transgender students from a local college joined the students and parents in the protest. Local residents spoke up about past productions of *Oklahoma!* and scoffed at the district's objections based on "mature adult themes." The school district held a meeting, and the room was filled beyond capacity, almost completely by people speaking up against the school's decision. The outcome: The school board voted unanimously to reinstate the musical and restore the original casting.

Valerie Fox, an LGBTQ+ advocate and parent of a queer student, noted, "What you're seeing today is history." Responding to the scene of dozens of transgender people and their supporters holding signs and flags outside the district office, she added, "This is one of the biggest things we've seen in Sherman." Max Hightower, the trans high school senior who had been cast in the lead role, exclaimed, "I'm beyond excited and everyone cried tears of joy." And a couple whose daughter lost her part playing a male character shared, "We were both nervous, because we live in Sherman," but when they saw the crowds gathering to protest the school's decision, "We began weeping"[6] tears of joy. This was a phenomenal and successful change effort, emblematic of the sweeping changes occurring around gender, even in small conservative towns in Texas. The good trouble in Sherman involved no civil disobedience, no violence. Instead, it was simply the coming together of a community of people in a small town to make a change, right a wrong, and get those youth of all genders back on stage—a coming together that made national news. Yes, we think we've crossed a threshold.

One town in Texas making good trouble cannot a revolution make. But when we look at other evidence, there is no doubt that a dramatic historical shift has occurred. We have the proliferation of programs to serve gender creative children and their families. Parents and Friends of Lesbian and Gays (PFLAG) has chapters all across the US. PFLAG was first established in 1973 in New York City by a small group of parents of gay and lesbian youth. Since that time, the PFLAG model has gone global, with similar affiliated organizations in Australia, Belgium, Canada, China, France, Israel, Jamaica, Japan, Mexico, Portugal, Spain, Switzerland, Uganda, the United Kingdom, and Vietnam. While PFLAG was first started as a place where parents, families, and allies of gay people could come together to find support, the organization now finds their chapter members swelling with parents and families of gender-diverse and transgender children who are also able to find incredible support there. Pediatric interdisciplinary gender programs, many of them situated in major hospitals, are only growing, even in the face of concerted efforts to close them down or restrict them. The World Professional Association for Transgender Health (WPATH), which started many decades ago by a small group of medical professionals, is now an international organization with members of all professions across the globe and publishes the international standards of care for transgender people. Schools around the world include gender as a key component of their diversity curriculum and prevail even in the face of challenges from groups wanting to ban books and curtail gender literacy.

Can a Gender Revolution Last?

Many revolutions are squelched. Others set the stage for a whole new world—as when the American Revolution transformed the United States from a British colony to an independent republic. What about this new gender revolution? We've become painfully aware that a cadre of, might we say, gender counterrevolutionaries are rallying hard to quash it. We have also come to recognize that these folks are mobilizing not because the gender revolution is on its last legs, ready to topple over, but because all of us involved in it—either as youth, parents, providers, citizens—have been responsible for its ascendance. When four pediatric clinics expand to over sixty within a decade in the US, something is clearly afoot.

Throw a dart at a date in history and you will discover a zeitgeist: The spirit of the age, the invisible force or agent dominating the characteristic of a given era in world history. It would not be far-fetched to assert that gender has become a central component of the Western zeitgeist as the twenty-first century has rolled out. Whether you support the concept of gender in all its variations or see it as a threat to be stopped, hardly a day goes by without reference to a gender-related issue across all media outlets. Who would ever have predicted that in 2022 *The New York Times* would devote three and a half pages and the front page feature to a discussion of puberty blockers? How many other times in history has a major daily newspaper paid that much attention to medical interventions that apply to less than 1 percent of the population, with all of those less-than-one percenters being children?

Over the course of history, we've learned that revolutions are never a static phenomenon. So, what can we imagine for the future of the present gender revolution? Recall that both of us authoring this book have aged out of any youth revolution. But that does not mean we aren't part of a larger movement in which that revolution is embedded. In the 1960s, we challenged gender roles and gender appearances—girls could be doctors, boys could be nurses, boys could grow their hair long and wear beads, girls could grow up to wear flannel shirts and overalls. In the 1970s, we fought for gay and lesbian rights. In the 1980s and 1990s, we fought for marriage equality. In the twenty-first century, we march, some of us now with canes or walkers, under the rainbow banner where all genders and all sexualities are welcome. At the head of the march are the children.

As two authors and psychologists, representing our profession and welcoming everyone under the rainbow banner, we hope that you, the readers, have come to see gender-affirmative providers as your friends who want to hear your concerns, answer your questions, and learn from you as you learn from us. When groups of us got together to assemble the gender-affirmative model of care for children of all genders, we never imagined that we would end up being accused of being wizards or rubber stampers: wizards who have the power to turn boys into girls and girls into boys; rubber stampers who need only hear one sentence coming from the mouth of a youth to give them the green light to legally change their name and gender marker and receive medical interventions—be it puberty suppression, gender-affirming hormones, even surgeries. We can say with assurance, that unlike Cinderella's fairy godmother who could turn a pumpkin into a carriage, no provider possesses a magic wand that can transform boys into girls or girls into boys. The only person who holds that power is the child themself as they spin their own unique gender web. As for being rubber stampers, regretfully, we cannot say with the same assurance that no provider has ever rubber-stamped a youth's gender requests without first taking a deep dive to listen, understand, and get that youth's gender in focus, with a goal of setting up a positive gender health plan. For those providers, we hope they will take in our perspective and join us in being neither wizards nor rubber stampers but friends of gender, and could we say, participants in the post-revolutionary world of gender, occasionally making good trouble.

Many of us have worked hard to find ways to teach children to be respectful of people of all races and religions. In the new zeitgeist of gender, we feel the urgency to put the same effort into teaching all our children to be respectful of people of all gender identities and expressions as well as creating a world for them in which we can all weave together our own unique gender selves, whether we are two or eighty years old.

Imagine

In 1971, John Lennon released the song *Imagine*, which indeed captured the imagination and the spirit of a whole generation of young people, and future generations to come. For those of us who listened to the song over and over, the message became etched in our brains, never to be forgotten—that we dream, join together, and create a world that will live as one.

What can we imagine in our future world of gender, one in which we hope we can grow closer to all and peacefully live as one? We can imagine a world with more scientific evidence about gender origins, gender pathways, and gender outcomes. We can imagine medical advances that create even more opportunities for people to live contentedly in the gender they know to be theirs. Perhaps uterine transplants will give trans women the opportunity to have a child or advanced reproductive techniques that don't rely on ova or sperm but rather cells from any body that can be stimulated to be reproductive cells, will allow people of all genders to couple and have babies together in a union of their two bodies, if they so choose. We can imagine the withering of false information as gender anxiety dwindles and people adjust to the revolutionary changes in gender that have already been set in motion, that are here to stay, and have the potential to bring peace on earth rather than dystopian disaster.

In 1992, James Carville, political consultant and campaign manager for Bill Clinton's first presidential campaign, coined the phrase "It's the economy, stupid," to rally campaign workers into action. Borrowing from that era, perhaps the new rallying cry should be, "It's the gender thing" (let's leave out the "stupid" part). Gender indeed has become a thing—to be explored, imagined, lived, and never taken for granted. We leave this book with the hope of having shed some light on the explosion of gender creativity, liberation of gender identities and expressions, and ever-expanding gender pathways. Let's imagine transcending gender as revolution for a time when gender in all its splendor is just a fact of life. We've identified obstacles to overcome as we move toward a world that is gender wonderful not just for some, but for all. To sustain ourselves until then, imagine a world with room for every gender under the sun.

Notes

Chapter 1: Much Ado About Gender

1. Vic Parsons, "Inventor of the Gender Reveal Party Regrets 'Creating a Monster' Now that She's Mother to a Gender Non-Conforming Kid," Pink News, June 29, 2020, thepinknews.co.uk/2020/06/29/gender-reveal-party-first-inventor-mother-jenna-karvunidis-monster-daughter.

2. Brandon Voss, "Creator of Gender-Reveal Parties Has Child Who Ignores Gender Norms," LogoTV, July 27, 2019.

3. Jody L. Herman et al., "How Many Adults and Youth Identify as Transgender in the United States?," UCLA School of Law The Williams Institute, June 2022, williamsinstitute.law.ucla.edu/publications/trans-adults-united-states.

4. Anna Brown, "About 5% of Young Adults in the U.S. Say Their Gender is Different from Their Sex Assigned at Birth," Pew Research Center, June 7, 2022, pewresearch.org/short-reads/2022/06/07/about-5-of-young-adults-in-the-u-s-say-their-gender-is-different-from-their-sex-assigned-at-birth.

5. Lucia He, "Latin America: The Most Deadly Region for Transgender Communities," Equal Times, November 16, 2016, equaltimes.org/latin-america-the-most-deadly.

6. Kate Lyons, "Gender Identity Clinic Services Under Strain as Referral Rates Soar," *The Guardian*, July 10, 2016.

7. Chantal M. Wiepjes et al., "The Amsterdam Cohort of Gender Dysphoria Study (1972–2015): Trends in Prevalence, Treatment, and Regrets," *Journal of Sexual Medicine* 15, no. 4 (2018): 582–90.

8. "10x Growth in Referrals to Gender Clinics in Canada and Our 'Consent' Based Model," Canadian Gender Report, May 18, 2021, genderreport.ca/10x-growth-in-referrals-to-gender-clinics-in-canada-and-our-consent-based-model.

9. Matt Lavietes, "From Book Bans to 'Don't Say Gay' Bill, LGBTQ Kids Feel 'Erased' in the Classroom," NBC News, February 20, 2022, nbcnews.com/nbc-out/out-news/book-bans-dont-say-gay-bill-LGBTQ-kids-feel-erased-classroom-rcna15819.

10. "Singular They," American Psychological Association, last updated July 2022, apastyle.apa.org/style-grammar-guidelines/grammar/singular-they.

11. "India Court Recognises Transgender People as Third Gender," BBC News, April 15, 2014, bbc.com/news/world-asia-india-27031180.

12. M. Mahbub Hossain et al., "Global Burden of Mental Health Problems Among Children and Adolescents During COVID-19 Pandemic: An Umbrella Review," *Journal of Psychiatric Research* 317, no. 114814 (2022).

13. Centers for Disease Control and Prevention, "Fatal Injury and Violence Data," in Jennifer L. Hughes et al., "Suicide in Young People: Screening, Risk Assessment, and Intervention," *BMJ* 381, no. e070630 (2023).

14. Asha Z. Ivey-Stephenson et al., "Suicidal Ideation and Behaviors Among High School Students—Youth Risk Behavior Survey, United States, 2019," *Supplements* 69, no. 1 (2020): 47–55.

15. "Teen Suicide Rates 'On the Rise,'" Suicide Bereavement UK, September 28, 2022, suicidebereavementuk.com/teen-suicide-rates-on-the-rise.

16. Jonah DeChants et al., "Homelessness and Housing Instability Among LGBTQ+ Youth," The Trevor Project, 2021, thetrevorproject.org/wp-content/uploads/2022/02/Trevor-Project-Homelessness-Report.pdf.

17. Emily M. Pariseau et al., "The Relationship Between Family Acceptance-Rejection and Transgender Youth Psychosocial Functioning," *Clinical Practice in Pediatric Psychology* 7, no. 3 (2019): 267–77.

18. Heather Havrilesky, "My Kid is Nonbinary, and I Can't Get Over It," The Cut, September 4, 2019, thecut.com/2019/09/ask-polly-my-kid-is-nonbinary-and-i-cant-get-over-it.html.

19. G. Nic Rider et al., "The Gender Affirmative Lifespan Approach (GALA): A Framework for Competent Clinical Care with Nonbinary Clients," *International Journal of Transgenderism* 20, nos. 2–3 (2019): 275–88.

20. Ibid.

21. Voss, op. cit.

Chapter 2: Why Is Gender a Thing for So Many Kids?

1. Anne Fausto-Sterling, *Sexing the Body: Gender Politics and the Construction of Sexuality* (New York: Basic Books, 2000).

2. Daphna Joel et al., "Sex beyond the genitalia: The human brain mosaic," *PNAS* 112, no. 50, (2015): 15468–73.

3. Diane Ehrensaft, *Gender Born, Gender Made: Raising Healthy Gender-Nonconforming Children* (New York: The Experiment, 2011); Diane Ehrensaft, *The Gender Creative Child: Pathways for Nurturing and Supporting Children Who Live Outside Gender Boxes* (New York: The Experiment, 2016).

4. Jeanne Maglaty, "When Did Girls Start Wearing Pink?," *Smithsonian* magazine, April 7, 2011.

5. Bob Johansen, *Full-Spectrum Thinking: How to Escape Boxes in a Post-Categorical Future* (Oakland, CA: Berrett-Koehler Publishers Inc, 2020).

6. Ehrensaft, *Gender Born, Gender Made*, op. cit.; Ehrensaft, *The Gender Creative Child*, op. cit.

Chapter 3: Why Does Gender Make People So Anxious?

1. Daniel Kahneman, *Thinking, Fast and Slow* (New York: Farrar, Straus & Giroux, 2011).

2. Emma Bryce, "How many calories can the brain burn by thinking?" Live Science, November 9, 2019, livescience.com/burn-calories-brain.html.

3. "What is Gender Dysphoria?" American Psychiatric Association, August 2022, psychiatry.org/patients-families/gender-dysphoria/what-is-gender-dysphoria.

4. "National Survey on LGBTQ Youth Mental Health 2020," The Trevor Project, 2020, thetrevorproject.org/wp-content/uploads/2020/07/The-Trevor-Project-National-Survey-Results-2020.pdf.

5. Ibid.

6. Serena Sonoma, "10 Transgender and Nonbinary People Explain What Gender Dysphoria Feels Like," last updated July 5, 2021, Daily Dot, dailydot.com/irl/gender-dysphoria.

7. Jack L. Turban et al., "Pubertal Suppression for Transgender Youth and Risk of Suicidal Ideation," *Pediatrics* 145, no. 2 (2022): e20191725.

8. Ibid.

9. Annelou L. C. de Vries et al., "Puberty Suppression in Adolescents With Gender Identity Disorder: A Prospective Follow-Up Study," *The Journal of Sexual Medicine* 8, no. 8 (2011): 2276–83, doi.org/10.1016/j.jadohealth.2021.10.036.

10. Ibid.

11. Ibid.

12. Luke Allen et al., "Well-Being and Suicidality Among Transgender Youth After Gender-Affirming Hormones," *Clinical Practice in Pediatric Psychology* 7, no. 3 (2019): 302–11.

13. Ibid.

14. de Vries et al., op. cit.

15. Turban et al., op. cit.

16. Ibid.

17. Azeen Ghorayshi, "How a Small Gender Clinic Landed in a Political Storm," *The New York Times*, last updated August 29, 2023, nytimes.com/2023/08/23/health/transgender-youth-st-louis-jamie-reed.html.

18. Evan Urquhart, "You Betrayed Us, Azeen," Assigned, September 3, 2023, assignedmedia.org/breaking-news/you-betrayed-us-azeen-parents-of-trans-youth-reeling-after-speaking-to-the-nyt.

19. Radhika Gharpure et al., "Knowledge and Practices Regarding Safe Household Cleaning and Disinfection for COVID-19 Prevention—United States, May 2020," *MMWR Morbidity and Mortality Weekly Report* 69, no. 23 (2020): 705–9.

20. "2023 Anti-Trans Bills Tracker," Trans Legislation Tracker, translegislation.com/bills/2023. Accessed October 2023.

21. "Map: Attacks on Gender Affirming Care By State," Human Rights Campaign, hrc.org/resources/attacks-on-gender-affirming-care-by-state-map. Accessed October 2023.

22. Ibid.

23. "Issues Impacting LGBTQ Youth: Polling Presentation," The Trevor Project, January 2023, thetrevorproject.org/wp-content/uploads/2023/01/Issues-Impacting-LGBTQ-Youth-MC-Poll_Public-2.pdf.

24. Kinzi Sparks, "New Data Illuminates Mental Health Concerns Among Texas' Transgender Youth Amid Record Number of Anti-Trans Bills," The Trevor Project, September 27, 2021, thetrevorproject.org/blog/new-data-illuminates-mental-health-concerns-among-texas-transgender-youth-amid-record-number-of-anti-trans-bills.

25. James Factora, "Hate Crimes Against Trans and Gender Nonconforming People Increased by 25% in 2022," Them, MSN, October 18, 2023, msn.com/en-us/news/us/hate-crimes-against-trans-and-gender-nonconforming-people-increased-by-25-in-2022/ar-AA1islTp.

26. "The Epidemic of Violence Against the Transgender and Gender Nonconforming Community in the United States: The 2023 Report," Human Rights Campaign Foundation, November 2023, reports.hrc.org/an-epidemic-of-violence-2023.

27. "Nonbinary and Transgender Californians Suffered Alarming Levels of Physical, Sexual Violence in the Past Year: Survey," Medical Press, September 6, 2023, medicalxpress.com/news/2023-09-nonbinary-transgender-californians-alarming-physical.html.

28. Amy Schwabe, "Trans kids in Wisconsin say a supportive network is critical in helping them face challenges from school policies, legislation and more," Milwaukee Journal Sentinel, October 11, 2023, jsonline.com/story/series/kidsincrisis/2023/10/11/transgender-youth-in-wisconsin-speak-out-on-importance-of-gender-affirmation/70900104007.

29. Kellan E. Baker, "The Future of Transgender Coverage," *New England Journal of Medicine*, 376, no. 19 (2017): 1801–4.

Chapter 4: What About This Gender-Affirmative Model?

1. Marco A. Hidalgo et al., "The gender affirmative model: What we know and what we aim to learn [Editorial]," *Human Development* 56, no. 5, (2013): 285–90.

2. The complete list of authors from the first four pediatric gender clinics in the US included Diane Chen, Leslie Clark, Diane Ehrensaft, Robert Garafolo, Marco Hidalgo, Johanna Olson, Stephen Rosenthal, Norman Spack, and Amy Tishelman.

3. Colt Keo-Meier and Diane Ehrensaft, *The Gender Affirmative Model: An Interdisciplinary Approach to Supporting Transgender and Gender Expansive Children* (Washington, DC: APA Publications, 2018).

4. Peggy T. Cohen-Kettenis and Friedemann Pfäfflin, *Transgenderism and Intersexuality in Childhood and Adolescence: Making Choices* (Thousand Oaks, CA: Sage, 2003).

5. Tony Bravo, "Barbie wasn't just a girls toy," *San Francisco Chronicle Sunday Datebook*, July 23–29, 2023, G6–9.

6. Soleil Ho, "I attended a secretive anti-trans dinner in San Francisco. And then I puked," *San Francisco Chronicle*, May 28, 2023, D2.

7. Diane Chen et al., "Psychosocial Functioning in Transgender Youth after 2 Years of Hormones," *The New England Journal of Medicine* 388, no. 3 (2023): 240–50.

8. Katherine G. Spencer et al., "The gender-affirmative life span approach: a developmental model for clinical work with transgender and gender-diverse children, adolescents, and adults," *Psychotherapy* 58, no. 1 (2021): 37–49.

Chapter 5: Where Have All the Young Girls Gone?

1. Abigail Shrier, *Irreversible Damage: The Transgender Craze Seducing Our Daughters* (New York: Regnery, 2020).

2. Lisa Littman, "Parent reports of adolescents and young adults perceived to show signs of a rapid onset of gender dysphoria," *PloS One* 13, no. 8 (2018): e0202330.

3. Lisa Littman, "Correction: Parent reports of adolescents and young adults perceived to show signs of a rapid onset of gender dysphoria," *PloS One* 14, no. 3 (2019): e0214157.

4. Timmy Broderick, "Evidence Undermines 'Rapid Onset Gender Dysphoria' Claims," *Scientific American*, August 24, 2023, scientificamerican.com/article/evidence-undermines-rapid-onset-gender-dysphoria-claims.

5. Greta R. Bauer et al., "Do Clinical Data from Transgender Adolescents Support the Phenomenon of 'Rapid Onset Gender Dysphoria'?," *The Journal of Pediatrics* 243 (2022): 224–27.

6. "CAAPS Position Statement on Rapid Onset Gender Dysphoria (ROGD)," Coalition for the Advancement & Application of Psychological Science, July 26, 2021, caaps.co/rogd-statement.

7. "Chapter 3: The Coming Out Experience," Pew Research Center, June 13, 2013, pewresearch.org/social-trends/2013/06/13/chapter-3-the-coming-out-experience.

8. "Homelessness and Housing Instability Among LGBTQ Youth," The Trevor Project, February 3, 2022, thetrevorproject.org/research-briefs/homelessness-and-housing-instability-among-LGBTQ-youth-feb-2022.

9. Oliver L. Haimson and Tiffany C. Veinot, "Coming Out to Doctors, Coming Out to 'Everyone': Understanding the Average Sequence of Transgender Identity Disclosures Using Social Media Data," *Transgender Health* 5, no. 3 (2020): 158–65.

10. Hal Boyle, "Rock 'n' Roll rhythm is sweeping the teen-age set, but what is it?" *Rapid City Journal*, April 4, 1955, quoted in "Rock 'n' roll music in the 50s: First adults called it a fad, then they wanted it banned," Click Americana, January 8, 2021, clickamericana. com/eras/1950s/rock-n-roll-music-in-the-50s.

11. Shrier, op. cit.

12. Annelies E. van Eeden et al., "Incidence, Prevalence and Mortality of Anorexia Nervosa and Bulimia Nervosa," *Current Opinion in Psychiatry* 34, no. 6 (2021): 515–24.

13. David A. Levy and Paul R. Nail, "Contagion: A Theoretical and Empirical Review and Reconceptualization," *Genetic Social and General Psychology Monographs* 119, no. 2 (1993): 233–84.

14. Broderick, op. cit.

15. Jack L. Turban et al., "Sex Assigned at Birth Ratio Among Transgender and Gender Diverse Adolescents in the United States," *Pediatrics* 150, no. 3 (2022).

16. Amelia Gentleman, "New NHS Children's Gender Clinic Hit by Disagreements and Resignations," *The Guardian*, January 18, 2024.

17. Chantal M. Wiepjes et al., "The Amsterdam Cohort of Gender Dysphoria Study (1972–2015): Trends in Prevalence, Treatment, and Regrets," *Journal of Sexual Medicine* 15, no. 4 (2018): 582–90.

18. Michelle M. Johns et al., "Transgender Identity and Experiences of Violence Victimization, Substance Use, Suicide Risk, and Sexual Risk Behaviors Among High School Students—19 States and Large Urban School Districts, 2017," *Morbidity Mortality Weekly Report* 68, no. 3 (2019): 67–71.

19. Alyssa L. Norris and Lindsay M. Orchowski, "Peer Victimization of Sexual Minority and Transgender Youth: A Cross-Sectional Study of High School Students," *Psychology of Violence* 10, no. 2 (2020): 201–11.

20. Gemma L. Witcomb et al., "Experiences and Psychological Wellbeing Outcomes Associated with Bullying in Treatment-Seeking Transgender and Gender-Diverse Youth," *LGBT Health* 6, no. 5 (2019).

21. "Separation and Stigma: Transgender Youth & School Facilities," Movement Advancement Project and GLSEN, April 2017, glsen.org/sites/default/files/2019-11/Separation_and_Stigma_2017.pdf.

22. Witcomb et al., op. cit.

23. Melissa Block, "'It's Hurtful': Trans Youth Speaks Out as Alabama Debates Banning Medical Treatment," NPR, March 28, 2021, npr.org/2021/03/28/981225604/its-hurtful-trans-youth-speaks-out-as-alabama-debates-banning-medical-treatment.

24. Jack L. Turban et al., "Gender Dysphoria and Gender Incongruence," in Andrés Martin et al. (eds.), *Lewis's Child and Adolescent Psychiatry: A Comprehensive Textbook, 5th Edition* (LWW, 2017), 632–43.

25. Kristina R. Olson et al., "Gender Identity 5 Years After Social Transition," *Pediatrics* 150, no. 2 (2022).

26. Christina Roberts, "Persistence of Transgender Gender Identity Among Children and Adolescents," *Pediatrics* 150, no. 2 (2022).

27. Ibid.

28. Jack L. Turban et al., "Factors Leading to 'Detransition' Among Transgender and Gender Diverse People in the United States: A Mixed-Methods Analysis," *LGBT Health* 8, no. 4 (2021): 273–80.

29. Valeria P. Bustos et al., "Regret After Gender-Affirmation Surgery: A Systemic Review and Meta-Analysis of Prevalence," *Plastic and Reconstructive Surgery Global Open* 9, no. 3 (2021).

30. Ana Wilson et al., "Regret in Surgical Decision Making: A Systematic Review of Patient and Physician Perspectives," *World Journal of Surgery* 41, no. 6 (2017): 1454–65.

31. Bustos et al., op. cit.

Chapter 6: Teach Your Parents Well: The Children Speak

1. "LGBTQ+ Advocates Sue Tennessee to Block Dangerous Transgender Healthcare Ban," Lambda Legal, April 20, 2023, lambdalegal.org/newsroom/tn_20230420_lgbtq-advocates-sue-tennessee-to-block-dangerous-transgender-healthcare-ban.

2. Ernesto Londono, "Conflict over Transgender Care Brings Statehouse to a Standstill," *The New York Times*, April 1, 2023, A1.

3. Ibid.

4. Ibid.

5. Robert Booth, "Less than Half in Britain Back Gender-Affirming Care for Trans Teenagers," *The Guardian*, June 8, 2023, theguardian.com/society/2023/jun/08/less-than-half-in-britain-back-gender-affirming-care-for-trans-teenagers.

6. John Bowlby, *Attachment and Loss: Attachment (vol. 1)*, 2nd edition (New York: Basic Books, 1999); M. D. Ainsworth, "Patterns of attachment behavior shown by the infant in interaction with his mother," *Merrill–Palmer Quarterly of Behavior and Development*, 10, no. 1 (1964): 51–58.

7. D. W. Winnicott, *The Family and Individual Development* (London: Tavistock Publications, 1978).

8. Selma H. Fraiberg, *The Magic Years: Understanding and Handling the Problems of Early Childhood* (New York: Charles Scribner's Sons, 1959).

9. Erik H. Erikson, *Childhood and Society* (New York: W. W. Norton & Company, 1950).

10. Colt Keo-Meier and Diane Ehrensaft, *The Gender Affirmative Model: An Interdisciplinary Approach to Supporting Transgender and Gender Expansive Children* (Washington, DC: APA Publications, 2018).

Chapter 7: What's a Parent to Do?

1. Caitlin Ryan et al., "Family Acceptance in Adolescence and the Health of LGBT Young Adults," *Journal of Child and Adolescent Psychiatric Nursing* 23, no. 4 (2010): 205–13; Sabra L. Katz-Wise et al., "Family Functioning and Mental Health of Transgender and Gender-Nonconforming Youth in the Trans Teen and Family Narratives Project," *The Journal of Sex Research* 55, no. 4–5 (2018): 582–90; Robb Travers et al., "Impacts of Strong Parental Support for Trans Youth," *Trans Pulse*, Children's Aid Society of Toronto & Delisle Youth Services (2012).

2. Bonnie Garmus, *Lessons in Chemistry* (New York: Doubleday, 2022).

3. Emily Witt, "Passages," *The New Yorker*, October 16, 2023. 14–20.

4. Tey Meadow, *Trans Kids: Being Gendered in the Twenty-First Century* (Berkeley: University of California Press, 2018), 43.

5. Laurie Frankel, *This Is How It Always Is* (New York: Flatiron Books, 2017), 327.

Chapter 8: Gender Conundrums: Sports, Education, and Medicine

1. Moriah Balingit, "Kentucky's Lone Transgender Athlete Can't Play on the Team She Helped Start," *The Washington Post*, August 25, 2022, washingtonpost.com/education/2022/08/25/fischer-wells-trans-athlete-kentucky.

2. Ibid.

3. Joseph G. Kosciw et al., "The 2021 National School Climate Survey: The Experiences of LGBTQ+ Youth in Our Nation's Schools," GLSEN, 2022, glsen.org/sites/default/files/2022-10/NSCS-2021-Full-Report.pdf.

4. "The National Youth Sports Strategy," US Department of Health and Human Services, 2019, health.gov/sites/default/files/2019-10/National_Youth_Sports_Strategy.pdf.

5. Shoshana K. Goldberg and Thee Santos, "The Importance of Sports Participation for Transgender Youth," American Progress, March 18, 2021, americanprogress.org/article/fact-sheet-importance-sports-participation-transgender-youth.

6. Frankie de la Cretaz, "What It Looks Like When Trans Kids Are Simply Allowed to Play Sports," Self, August 24, 2023, self.com/story/trans-kids-playing-sports.

7. "The Well-Being of LGBTQ Youth Athletes," The Trevor Project, August 2020. www.thetrevorproject.org/wp-content/uploads/2020/08/LGBTQ-Youth-Sports-and-Well-Being-Research-Brief.pdf.

8. Ibid.

9. Kosciw et al., op. cit.

10. Shoshana K. Goldberg, "Fair Play: The Importance of Sports Participation for Transgender Youth," American Progress, February 2021, americanprogress.org/article/fair-play.

11. "YRBSS Data & Documentation," Centers for Disease Control and Prevention, last updated August 18, 2023, cdc.gov/healthyyouth/data/yrbs/data.htm.

12. "Bans on Transgender Youth Participation in Sports," Movement Advancement Project (MAP), lgbtmap.org/equality-maps/youth/sports_participation_bans. Accessed November 2023.

13. Goldberg, op. cit.

14. Kosciw et al., op. cit.

15. "What are the key takeaways from the new transgender guidance for schools?" itvNews, December, 19, 2023, itv.com/news/2023-12-19/what-are-the-key-takeaways-from-the-new-transgender-guidance-for-schools.

16. Robbie Meredith, "School Transgender Support Guidelines Published," BBC News, October 17, 2019, bbc.com/news/uk-northern-ireland-50076038.

17. R. Bethene Ervin et al., "Measures of Muscular Strength in U.S. Children and Adolescents, 2012," *NCHS Data Brief*, 139 (2013).

18. Jack Turban, "Trans Girls Belong on Girls' Sports Teams," *Scientific American*, March 16, 2021, scientificamerican.com/article/trans-girls-belong-on-girls-sports-teams.

19. Katrina Karkazis, quoted in Turban, op. cit.

20. Kristen Conti, "IOC Announces New Rules for Transgender Athletes Before Paris 2024 Olympics," NECN, December 20, 2022, necn.com/news/sports/ioc-announces-new-rules-for-transgender-athletes-before-paris-2024-olympics/2894329.

21. Balingit, op. cit.

22. Francesca Specter, "'It's an ongoing challenge': Will the culture wars come for Britain's books?," *The Independent*, December 2, 2023, independent.co.uk/life-style/book-bans-uk-us-censorship-b2456957.html.

23. David Reby et al., "Sex stereotypes influence adults' perception of babies' cries," *BMC Psychology* 4, no. 19 (2016).

24. Schuyler Bailar, *He/She/They: How We Talk About Gender and Why It Matters* (New York: Hachette Book Group, 2023).

25. Janet Y. Lee and Stephen M. Rosenthal, "Gender-Affirming Care of Transgender and Gender-Diverse Youth: Current Concepts," *Annual Review of Medicine* 74 (2023): 107–16.

26. M. A. T. C. van der Loos et al., "Bone mineral density in transgender adolescents treated with puberty suppression and subsequent gender-affirming hormones," *JAMA Pediatrics* 177, no. 12 (2023): 1332–41.

27. Giulia Giacomelli and Maria Cristina Meriggiola, "Bone Health in Transgender People: A Narrative Review," *Therapeutic Advances in Endocrinology and Metabolism* 13 (2022).

28. Robin Respaut and Chad Terhune, "Putting Numbers on the Rise in Children Seeking Gender Care," Reuters, October 6, 2022, reuters.com/investigates/special-report/usa-transyouth-data.

29. Valeria P. Bustos et al., "Regret After Gender-Affirmation Surgery: A Systemic Review and Meta-Analysis of Prevalence," *Plastic and Reconstructive Surgery Global Open* 9, no. 3 (2021).

30. Ana Wilson et al., "Regret in Surgical Decision Making: A Systematic Review of Patient and Physician Perspectives," *World Journal of Surgery* 41, no. 6 (2017): 1454–65.

Chapter 9: Through the Looking Glass

1. Diane Ehrensaft, *Gender Born, Gender Made: Raising Healthy Gender-Nonconforming Children* (New York: The Experiment, 2011).

2. University of California, Osher Lifelong Learning Institute, olli.berkeley.edu.

3. Avgi Saketopoulou and Ann Pellegrini, *Gender Without Identity* (New York: Unconscious in Translation, 2023), 15.

4. Linda Graves, *Corey's Story*, January 30, 2014, unpublished manuscript.

Chapter 10: Gender Evolution to Revolution: What's Next?

1. Jason Horowitz, "Quiet Talks, Loud Defiance and Pontiff's Gift," *The New York Times*, December 22, 2023, A1–10.

2. Katherine Locke, *What Are Your Words? A Book About Pronouns* (New York: Little, Brown and Company, 2021).

3. John McWhorter, "Knowing When 'They Means One," *The New York Times*, November 28, 2023, A15.

4. Solcyré Burga, "U.K. Museum Says Roman Emperor Was a Trans Woman," *Time*, November 22, 2023.

5. John Lewis, "Together, You Can Redeem the Soul of Our Nation," *The New York Times*, July 30, 2020.

6. J. David Goodman, "In Texas, Fight over Gender and School Theater Takes an Unexpected Turn," *The New York Times*, November 18, 2023, A13.

Acknowledgments

So many people have made *Gender Explained* possible. First, we'd like to thank every child, every teen, and every family that we have had the pleasure of getting to know as we have worked as gender specialists over these many years. And then, a deep mutual thanks to each other—neither of us could have done this work alone and have had a gift in getting to do it together.

We also could not have birthed this book without the wisdom and commitment of all the staff at The Experiment who shepherded us through our writing from start to finish. A deep thanks to Matthew Lore, cofounder, president, and publisher at The Experiment and a person so deeply committed to getting the word out about gender creative children; to Batya Rosenblum, our brilliant executive editor who combed through every word and smoothed the rough edges to make each page speak as we hoped it would; Ally Mitchell, our wonderful and creative copy editor who did the second thorough combing beyond all our expectations; Besse Lynch, our publicist, for getting the word out that our book has been born ; Jack Dunnington, our cover designer, for dressing our book in its finest clothes; Zach Pace, our managing editor; and Juli Barbato, our proofreader.

Both of us would also like to especially thank all the members of Mind the Gap, our consortium of mental health gender specialists that we have both been involved in since its inception, with special thanks to the fellow members in our advisory group, Karisa Barrow,

Susan "Bernie" Bernstein, Shawn Giammattei. All of your collective wisdom runs through every page of *Gender Explained*.

For Diane: This book could never have been born without the inspiration, wisdom, and friendship of my coauthor, Michelle. There is no way I could thank her enough.

And I could never have learned about gender-diverse youth, and continue to learn about them to this day, without my wonderful community and interdisciplinary team at the UCSF Benioff Children's Hospital Child and Adolescent Gender Center (CAGC). I don't know how to even begin to thank Stephen Rosenthal, cofounder with me and others of the CAGC, our Medical Director, and my partner and close friend in every step of our own gender-affirmative journey. I will never stop learning from you. And to the rest of our team, past and present—Chase Anderson, Kristin Avicolli, Joel Baum, Tina Chaffin, Abby Cobb-Walch, Jessie Rose Cohen, Tracy Estrada Marquez, Catherine Fuller, Chelsea Garnett, Shawn Giammattei, Dan Karasic, Molly Koren, Jess Kremen, Janet Lee, Rae Liberto, Kobi Mar, Matthew Meyers, Blair Neuman, Logan Paracuelles, Andrea Pedersen, Meredith Russell, Herb Schrier, Ilana Sherer, Jack Turban—you are the best professional family anyone could ask for.

A great indebtedness, too, to members of our multisite NIH research team—Yee Ming Chan, Diane Chen, Mona Desai, Robert Garafolo, Misha Kaufman, Marco Hidalgo, Julie McAvoy-Banerjea, Johanna Olson-Kennedy, Annarose Peck-Block, Hanno Petra, Stephen Rosenthal (mentioned again), and most importantly, my wonderful study coordinator at UCSF, Molly Seligman, for walking the walk with evidence-based scientific research so we can find out if the kids are fine.

No explaining could be done without my "gender gang"—wonderful friends and colleagues around the country who have been there every step of the gender-affirmative way—Mere Abrams, Lin Fraser, Ben Geilhufe, Jen Hastings, Shane Hill, Linda Hawkins, Sabra Katz-Wise, Lisette Lahana, Ximena Lopez, Jean Malpas, Francie Mandel, Susanna Moore, Scott Mosser, Simon Pickstone-Taylor, Megan

Smith, Kelley Storck, Amy Tishelman. And my team members writing the childhood chapter for the WPATH Standards of Care Version 8—Dianne Berg, Laura Edwards-Leeper, Susie Green, Aron Janssen, Jiska Ristori, Tomas Steensma, John Strang, Amy Tishelman (again). And my coeditors in the upcoming revised edition of *The Gender Affirmative Model*, Nic Rider and Colt St. Amand.

Gender never stands on its own and is embedded in so many areas of life. Deepest thanks to my child consultation group, old and new— Lea Brown, Eileen Keller, Piera Piagentini, Bonnie Rottier, Stephen Walrod. And to my "besties," friends and fellow psychologists—Victor Bonfilio, Ghislaine Boulanger, Ruth Fallenbaum, Toni Heineman, Gloria Lawrence, Maureen Murphy, Stephanie Riger, Milton Shaefer, Marsha Silverstein for nurturing me to think and feel both inside and outside myself.

Lastly, family. First my chosen one of many, many years: Elli and Robby Meeropol, Joanna Levine and Mark Stickgold, Randy Reiter and Joan Skolnick, Nancy Hollander and Stephen Portuges, Joel Crohn and Mindy Werner-Crohn, Anne Bernstein and Ringo Hallinan, Nancy Chodorow and Carl Salzman. You have all helped me so much get from here to there and beyond. And my "blood ties" family. No one could have been luckier than me to have your circle of love around me—my brother and sister-in-law, Rick Ehrensaft and Linda Lofton, my brother Phil Ehrensaft, my two incredible children, Rebecca Hawley and Jesse Ehrensaft-Hawley, my beloved granddaughter, Satya Hawley, my parents, Edith and Morris Ehrensaft, no longer with us but always there in spirit, and the biggest hug to my husband, Jim Hawley, there every morning with a groggy smile to make my day.

For Michelle: In addition to being my coauthor, I want to offer a special thanks to Diane for her ongoing mentorship since the beginning of my work in pediatric gender care. You are someone who I never stop learning from. Deepest thanks to the youth who agreed to tell me their stories for this book—you know who you are. I want to thank Jack Turban for pointing me in the right direction to start my deep dive into this research. I also want to thank members of my clinical consultation group, Zoe Barnow and Hall McCann, for our generative meetings in which we think so well together and for your support whenever I needed it. And thank you to Susan "Bernie" Bernstein for being my colleague on our gender learning journey and for being my friend—your support and humor helps keep me going.

And thank you to all my loved ones and chosen family. I especially want to thank Meg Yardley for always being there—whether through your patient edits, constructive feedback, or just your company and support over the decades. Thank you to Chris and Sharise Quinby for being my consistent cheerleaders throughout this process. I am grateful to call you family. Much gratitude to Janis Bishop, for your unwavering support and for helping me to meet life's challenges with grace. I am also grateful for Joann Driscoll for your always ready ear, understanding, and support. Thank you to Aunt Gloria—you are living testament that underneath contrasting viewpoints often lie similar desires. Of course, thank you to my mom for teaching me in my earliest years that difference is something to be celebrated and not feared. And finally, many thanks to my dad. Even though you no longer walk this earth, you live forever in my heart—thank you for teaching me the importance of standing up for truth and living with integrity in all that I do.

Index

beliefs and attitudes (*continued*)
  implicit biases, 15, 128,
    165–69, 172
  information seeking for
    reassurance, 41–42
  legislation and laws on
    gender, 53–55
  media and misinformation,
    50–52
  religious, 64, 167–68, 175–76
  social gender dysphoria and,
    55–57
Bianchi, Anna, 159
bias
  implicit, 15, 128, 165–69, 172
  of media, 51
  in research, 95–96
books
  bans of, 4, 148
  on pronouns, 177
Bowlby, John, 111
brain adaptability, 38–41
brain development, 26–27, 97
bullying, 47, 95–97, 149

C
Carpenter, Karen, 90–91
Centers for Disease Control
  and Prevention (CDC), 7,
  96, 144
child development, 115–16,
  119–20
children, listening to, 101–15
  developmental stages and,
    115–16

example from literature, 103–4
feedback loop with parents,
  111–13
gender-affirmative model of
  care and, 75–77
gender expression and, 64,
  75–77
gender expression stories,
  104–11
learning from children, 101–3
mirroring by parents, 113–15
cisgender people
  defined, xvii
  gender expression and, 21
cisnormative, 151
color choices, 1, 29, 101–3, 160
conversion therapy, 64
critical thinking, 133, 147, 150,
  173
culture, 19–36
  external pressure to re-
    transition and, 99
  feminist movement and
    changes in, 22, 24, 60
  full-spectrum thinking and,
    35–36
  gender as bedrock in, 8–9, 36,
    73, 121, 123
  gender as product of, 24, 27,
    64, 148–49, 177
  gender boxes and, 33–34
  gender dysphoria as response
    to, 45
  gender expression and shifts
    in, 23–24

gender norms, shifts in, 12,
13, 21–24, 28–32
gender revolution and,
31–33, 179–85
gender vs. sex in, 24–26
generation gap and, 31
nature vs. nurture and, 27,
119–20
sex ratio of transgender
youth and, 94–95
social gender dysphoria and,
55–57
trans girls vs. trans boys,
acceptance of, 19–20,
94–95

D

Department of Labor (US), 23
depression and anxiety
gender-affirming hormone
treatment and, 47–48, 151,
155
gender dysphoria and, 44,
47–48
negative social responses to
gender expression and, 63
sports participation and,
141–43
detransitioning, 97–99
DFAB (designated female at
birth), defined, xvii, 12–13
*Diagnostic and Statistical Manual
of Mental Disorders* (DSM-5-
TR), 42–44
Dìaz, Rafael, 126

discrimination
in employment, 32
mental health and, 57, 96
re-transition decisions based
on, 99
social gender dysphoria and,
56–57
sports, transgender youth
and, 139, 143
Wellesley College as safe
haven from, 22
disinformation, 50–52
DMAB (designated male at
birth), defined, xvii, 12–13
dual processing theory, 38–39
Duron, Lori, 119

E

eating disorders, 90–91
educational specialists, 70
Ehrensaft, Diane, 62, 65
Elagabalus (Roman Emperor),
178
*Emperor of Rome? Ruling the
Ancient Roman World* (Beard),
178
employment
gender-inclusive policies in,
23
gender norms and, 32
Endocrine Society, 77
endocrinologists, 71
estrogen therapy, 79, 95, 145,
155. *See also* hormone therapy

F

Fairness in Women's Sports Act (Kentucky, 2022), 139–40

family rejection
gender minority stress and, 21
housing instability and, 7, 88
mental health outcomes and, 84, 113–15, 126
self-harm and, 130
suicide risk and, 7

Feminine Mystique (Friedan), 104

femininity, 28–33

feminist movement, 22, 24, 31–32, 60

fertility, 79, 156

Follett, Mary Parker, 139

Fox, Valerie, 181

Fraiberg, Selma, 116, 131

Francis (pope), 175

Frankel, Laurie, 59, 138

Frankl, Viktor, 37

Freud, Sigmund, 119

Friedan, Betty, 104

full-spectrum thinking, 34–36, 72

G

GAHT. *See* gender-affirming hormone treatment

gay rights movement, 22, 32

gender. *See also* beliefs and attitudes; children, listening to; gender, future directions for; gender conundrums; parents; self-awareness; transgender youth
automatic assignment of, 39
beliefs and attitudes, 37–57. *See also* beliefs and attitudes
brain differences and, 26–27
children, listening to, 101–15. *See also* children, listening to
children learning about, 111–15, 131–35, 146–50, 173
as cultural construct, 24, 27, 64, 148–49, 177
defined, 26–27
future directions for, 175–83
gender-affirmative model of care, 59–82. *See also* gender-affirmative model of care
gender conundrums, 139–57. *See also* gender conundrums
historical shifts in behaviors and norms, 28–32
nature vs. nurture and, 27, 119–20
as organizing principle, 39–40
parents with gender creative kids, 119–38. *See also* parents

gender inclusivity
  as goal, 161
  in higher education, 22–23
  language for, 5–6, 23
  in schools, 70
  in sports, 140–46
gender literacy, 12, 133–34,
  147–50, 173
gender medical centers and
  programs, 3–4, 62, 69–71,
  93–94. *See also* gender-
  affirming medical care
gender minority stress. *See also*
  discrimination
  defined, xviii
  gender-affirmative model of
    care and, 69
  gender noise and, 47
  parents as source of, 21, 128
  puberty and, 20–21, 94, 156,
    169–70
  Rapid Onset Gender
    Dysphoria and, 86
  social gender dysphoria and,
    55–57
  sports for coping with, 141
gender neutrality, 23, 160–61
gender-neutral language, 5–6,
  23
gender noise, xviii, 47
gender norms. *See* culture;
  gender stereotypes and roles
genderqueer, defined, xviii
gender reveal parties, 1–2, 8,
  123

gender revolutions, 31–33,
  179–85
Gender Spectrum conferences,
  61
gender stereotypes and roles
  children learning about,
    147–50
  culture and conformity to,
    45
  gender differences in brain
    and, 26–27
  gender norms, shifts in, 12,
    13, 21–24, 28–32
  sexism and, 84
  theater assignments in
    schools and, 180–82
gender stress. *See* gender
  minority stress
gender terminology, 12–13
gender transitions
  medical, 97–99, 150–51
  social, 69–70, 151–53
gender web
  child development and, 116
  flexibility of, 162–63, 169
  influences on, 92, 112
  nature vs. nurture and,
    119–20
  overview, 27–28
  puberty and, 77–78
  social gender transitions and,
    152
  support from parents and,
    126
  unique to each person, 104

About the Authors

DIANE EHRENSAFT, PhD, is a developmental and clinical psychologist and the author of *The Gender Creative Child* and *Gender Born, Gender Made*. At the University of California, San Francisco, she is the cofounder and director of mental health at the Child and Adolescent Gender Center and an associate professor of pediatrics. She has been featured on the *Los Angeles Times* online and *WIRED* online and has appeared on *Anderson Live, The Oprah Winfrey Show*, and the *Today Show*.

dianeehrensaft.com

MICHELLE JURKIEWICZ, PsyD, is a licensed clinical psychologist and gender specialist in private practice in Berkeley, California. She has been providing therapeutic services to children, youth, and families since 2003. Dr. Jurkiewicz was an early pioneer in the work with transgender, nonbinary, and gender expansive youth. In addition to providing psychotherapy for people of all ages, she trains newer clinicians in using the gender-affirmative model.

stillwaterspsychotherapy.com